Hospitality
with Confidence

Hospitality
with Confidence

Grace Pittman

Dear Nina,

I hope you enjoy
this book & find
it practical

Love

Grace Pittman

II Cor. 4:7

BETHANY HOUSE PUBLISHERS
MINNEAPOLIS, MINNESOTA 55438
A Division of Bethany Fellowship, Inc.

Published by Bethany House Publishers
A Division of Bethany Fellowship, Inc.
6820 Auto Club Road, Minneapolis, Minnesota 55438

Printed in the United States of America

Library of Congress Cataloging-in-Publication Data

Pittman, Grace, 1927-
   Hospitality with confidence.

   Bibliography: p.
   1. Hospitality—Religious aspects—Christianity.
I. Title.

BV4647.H67P58   1986   241'.4   86-3609
ISBN 0-87123-858-6

To my longsuffering husband, Sam,
who has kept me moving on this project,
mixing just the right amount of
admonition and encouragement.
He has also borne with me on my
many experiments in the arena of hospitality.
Along the way he has helped me to have the
confidence needed for such an undertaking.

GRACE PITTMAN, wife and mother of two daughters, has served as a missionary for 17 years in Pakistan in a ministry among Muslim women. She presently works for the Midwestern office of the Conservative Baptist Foreign Mission and with Student Missions Fellowship on a university campus. She makes her home in St. Paul, Minnesota.

Table of Contents

Introduction

What do Betty Crocker, Ann Pillsbury, Gloria Vanderbilt, Emily Post, Julia Child, and Heloise have in common? The answer is obvious.

In this book I don't expect to compete with any one of them. I do, however, hope to approach the subject of entertaining and hospitality from a different angle, combining a little of each of these well-known women and their expertise.

But most important, I have one goal: to challenge Christians from all walks of life to plunge into the delightful practice of entertaining, of using their homes for someone other than themselves and their own families, experiencing what it means to share an "open home."

Whether to a Christian there is a fine point that distinguishes entertaining from the practice of hospitality, I really do not know. For the Christian, though, "entertaining" takes on a new meaning, one with spiritual overtones. I therefore care not whether you use the term "entertaining" or "having company" or "practicing hospitality." I *do* care that you get involved in this indispensable ministry.

This book has to do with the "how" of hospitality: gracious sharing, cooking, serving, menus, recipes, table decorating and napkin folding—none as ends in themselves, but all for the purpose of ministering through our homes to those around us, both Christians and non-Christians.

I have drawn most from my own mother, who for me epitomized true graciousness. I have drawn from many others as well—both from other hosts and from guests with whom we have shared our home.

I wish to thank all those who have taught me by principle and precept what it means to keep an open home. I want to thank my own parents (who are now truly at home with their heavenly Father), my wonderful stepmother, and my sisters, who also are known for their practice of hospitality.

I need to say a special thanks to Dr. Willard Scofield for getting me started on this project and asking about it often enough to keep me motivated. I should also mention Mrs. Eleanor Anderson, who proposed the idea of a seminar on the subject of "Hallowed Hospitality."

By far, the one who has helped the most has been my beloved husband, Sam. He has patiently but firmly kept me moving, prodding me here, pushing me there, rejoicing with me in each new accomplishment. Without him someone else would have had to write this book. Along with Sam, my two daughters and a handsome, terrific son-in-law never lost confidence in me and my ability to get this job done. So thanks to all.

Chapter One

Mold Behind the Shower Curtain

Hospitality from a biblical perspective is to recognize that God is more interested in caring relationships than the mold behind the shower curtain. . . . It need not matter if we live in a single-room apartment or a split-level ranch, the only real requirement is allowing God to use our lives and possessions. . . . Our homes and our lives are indeed the most powerful combination for ministry to our world."

When I first read that statement in a delightful little publication that comes to our home occasionally, it stopped me cold. I first thought, *Now that is a powerfully big statement—perhaps too big.* But the more I thought about it, the more unnerved I became. It reminded me of the mold behind my shower curtain. I consider myself a reasonably good housekeeper—at least things usually look in order on the surface (but only *I* know what is behind the closet and cupboard doors). I must confess, that though I enjoy cleaning the house, I have a bad habit of leaving the bathroom undone, a job I despise. I can't honestly remember whether the mold behind the shower curtain has ever kept me from inviting guests, but it is often a nagging worry. How big of a worry depends, of course, on who the guests are. Maybe my guests, or at least some of them, do go into the bathroom, lock the door, then look to see if there is mold behind the shower curtain. But, I can't worry about that.

That the size of a house is not important is another big statement. We don't live in a one-room apartment. Neither do we live in an elegant mansion. Ours is a normal, moderately sized Midwestern house, not elegant or fancy, but comfortable, nicely arranged, and, most important, it is ours (even though we're sharing it with the bank).

Actually, I believe this statement could be expanded. It not only doesn't matter what kind of house we live in, it doesn't matter whether we are young or old, male or female, single or married, parents or childless, permanently or temporarily settled. What really matters is that we belong to God. He is in us, living out His life through us. Not only do we belong to Him, but all we have, including our homes, belongs to Him. It really is true that our homes and our lives are the most powerful combination for ministry to our world. Of course there are other powerful combinations for ministry—our workplace and our lives, our relationships with other people and our lives. But our homes and our lives are a uniquely powerful combination.

We must ask ourselves a searching question: "If our homes and our lives really are the most powerful combination for ministry, then why do we so easily neglect this important aspect of Christianity?"

From the Scripture we can conclude that the practice of real Christian hospitality isn't an option. We are taught that to neglect its practice in some form or other is actually disobedience. In other words, hospitality is an integral part of the teaching of Scripture. Paul is forthright in his statement: "Practice hospitality" (Rom. 12:13, NIV). What could be clearer than that? Even Peter, in his epistle, doesn't mince words: "Offer hospitality to *one another* without grumbling" (1 Pet. 4:9, NIV). "Do I have to do it without grumbling, Lord?" we may ask. It seems that that command goes a bit too far. I wish I could honestly say I have always kept an open home without grumbling. Sometimes there is grumbling, but I go ahead and practice hospitality anyway.

I happen to be one Christian who would rather be encouraged than commanded to do something. I believe most people feel the same way. Scripture reminds us that "when you give a banquet, invite the *poor*, the *crippled*, the *lame*, the *blind*, and you will be blessed. Although they cannot repay you, you will be repaid at the resurrection of the righteous" (Luke 14:13, 14). I would like to ask Luke, "Do you mean to say that I am to invite people like that—people I know will not be able to repay me in any way? Am I really to open my home to that kind of people?" I already know the answer. That exhortation really gets under the skin.

The Epistle to the Hebrews urges us: "Do not forget to entertain *strangers*, for by so doing some people have entertained angels without knowing it." Notice how we have moved from the simple command to "one another," then on to the "poor, the crippled, the lame, the blind," and then on to "strangers." Most of us don't have any trouble extending love and care, even our homes, to the "one anothers" of God's family. The rest of the order is much bigger and more difficult.

Quite apart from the commands and encouragements given in Scripture, we also find examples that strike us like shafts of light, reminding us that even though hospitality may not be our practice, it has been the very fabric of everyday life from the early pages of the Bible. My favorite story of a man and wife willing to risk entertaining strangers is found in Genesis 18. Of course we know the deep inner meaning of this account, how God was accomplishing His purposes in the beginning days of Israel. We know that God used three strangers to tell Abraham he would have a son.

After living in the Eastern world for so long, the story has new meaning to me. Actually, it always elicits a chuckle. You see, it wasn't just a little thing when Abraham ran inside to spout off orders to Sarah. His leaving strangers outside in the hot sun perhaps tells us how frantic he was. If *he* was frantic, think how frustrated Sarah must have been at what Abraham asked her to do: "Quick, prepare three measures of fine flour, knead it, and make bread cakes." Sure, Abraham, that's an easy command for you to give. Have you ever tried to do what he asked her to do while three guests are waiting to be invited in? There are some things, like making bread, that just aren't done quickly. And things moved very slowly in those days. There was no supermarket, no refrigeration—and no frozen bread dough. Obviously, Abraham didn't fully understand what it was to be a housewife, what was involved in getting a meal on the table in a hurry.

I would have been more than a little frantic. Sarah must have taken comfort, though, in the fact that he at least helped—he didn't make her go out to the herd grazing behind the tent to find the right animal to be sacrificed on the altar of hospitality and propriety. He did that himself. The curds were perhaps on hand. But the fresh milk involved milking. According to Eastern tradition, this has to be a respectable meal, not just a snack. But Abraham and Sarah did what they had to do. And think of the blessing that came to them and what they would have missed had they not invited the strangers in. These unexpected, uninvited guests were the messengers of the Holy God!

I remember some we were tempted to turn away. They always came just before dawn, because in Karachi, where we lived, the planes always arrived in the middle of the night. Some felt so much at home with us that they usually came without warning. Of course many came without warning because there was no way to let us know. I remember well one such occasion. I was filling my washing machine when I heard a knock on the door. I ran to the door and found two strangers. I had never seen such a pitiful, bedraggled couple in my life. The dust on them told me they had been on a long train ride. They looked exhausted and my heart went out to them. Did I let them in? Of course I let them in. They were missionaries and they needed my attention urgently. So did the water running into the washing machine! When I got back to the laundry room, the long tongue of water was slowly creeping into the children's bedroom. Water was everywhere it wasn't supposed to be. What should I do? First, turn off the water. Next, get acquainted with these first-timers. I calmly put towels and mops into their hands and invited them into the bedroom. On our knees, mopping up the water, we got well acquainted. I encouraged them by saying they could have a nice cool shower in their very own bathroom and a nice nap in their very own bedroom under their very own fan. All that would be waiting for them when we had all the water cleaned up. They rose to the occasion with aplomb and the job was soon finished. They have become quite famous, and I never hear their names now without remembering them on their hands and knees mopping up the water. We were always very comfortable with each other. Their unexpected visit enriched our home beyond measure, and we were able to have a part in their adjustment to a strange, new culture. They came back many times after that, but they will always remember their first visit. Yes, they became good friends. Yet Scripture even goes beyond encouraging us to welcome those who might not come at the best time or who can't repay us.

I feel a bit unnerved about showing hospitality to people I might consider enemies. I don't think I have a lot of enemies, but you never can tell. Sure, there are those who are not my friends, but enemies? Not many. In 2 Kings 6, we find the strange story of Elisha and the king of Israel. They had the opportunity right at their fingertips to settle an old score by killing their enemies. When the king asked

Elisha if they should just get the job done and kill these enemies, Elisha replied as a true man of God: "You shall not kill them. Would you kill those you have taken captive with your sword and with your bow? Set bread and water before them, that they may eat and drink and go to their master. So he prepared a great feast for them; and when they had eaten and drunk he sent them away and they went to their master" (2 Kings 6:22, 23, NAS).

You're probably thinking that someone would have to be a super-saint to respond like that. None of us are super-saints. Even though we know our homes and everything in them are generous gifts from a loving heavenly Father, even though we know everything we have is to be shared with others, and even though we know everything the Bible teaches about this subject, we still manage to find excuses. The problem is, we not only neglect entertaining enemies and strangers, but we neglect those inside the family of God. We take the line of least resistance. We fret and fume when we know people are coming, and we fall apart when people come unexpectedly. We imagine ghastly things that never happen—well, almost never. We talk ourselves into the false notion that there are certain "personality types" who by nature love to entertain, and decide we're not like them. We rationalize that this simply is not our special "gift." We use very strange excuses: Our house isn't good enough; our house isn't big enough; our kids are too small; our teenagers act awful; we don't have time; we get too nervous; the house is a mess; the cupboards are a mess. In short, our excuses rob us of a myriad of blessings God wants to pour out as we serve other people.

We trip ourselves up by constantly looking at other people. In the practice of hospitality, creativity is the name of the game. There is absolutely no limit to what each of us, with our own resources, abilities, strengths, personality, and commitment, can do through our homes to minister to people. I believe each of us, rich or poor, educated or uneducated, smart or not-so-smart, low-keyed or keyed-up, can use our creative energy to transform our homes into places where other people can come and find blessing, peace and enjoyment.

What is a home? The definition of a home is "a place where one lives." It is a simple definition, but it includes everyone. We all have a home of one kind or another. For many of us that home includes other people—our family. For others, "home" means a place that is shared with a roommate, or several roommates or housemates. By the same token, a home is not just a place where there is a husband

and a wife, and children. A home is a dorm room, a basement apartment—anywhere where people live.

Here we have to reach beyond the picture of a family—mother, father and children—and emphasize that the practice of Christian hospitality in the home is not limited only to those who have taken the step of marriage. Of course in our culture, we are used to women being responsible for the fine art of hospitality. Cookbooks and magazines are geared to women—especially married women.

May I encourage you to consider that the heart of a servant is just as apt to be found in a man as in a woman—just as surely to be found in a single person, man or woman, as a married person. Men, too, need to be encouraged to become involved in hospitality. If it is easy for a woman to go to the supermarket and find items for a meal easy and quick to prepare, the same is true for a man. I think of all the young men I know who live in apartments, some alone and some with others. That apartment is every bit as appropriate a place to entertain guests as a home with husband, wife, and children. What a tremendous means of evangelism such a home could be. There is no reason why a single man can't get involved in this very satisfying ministry of hospitality as a tool for Christian witness. I have known many who have become very involved. Just recently we were invited to a dinner for about thirty guests in a lovely suburban home. The hostess did not prepare the meal. Rather, a young man who was getting ready to go to China to teach had asked if he could prepare the whole meal. This long, lanky China-bound child of God, with his tall chef's hat, wielding the knifes, stirring the food in the wok, and then serving it artistically from the large buffet table, was a sight to behold. No one can convince me that he was not enjoying himself and lapping up the praise given him. He loved every minute of it— a favorite avenue of service for him I learned later.

Further, it is also wonderful to see a couple, husband and wife, equally involved in preparing and serving a meal. How fortunate we are to be living in a time and in a culture where it is quite acceptable for a man to be involved in preparing and serving the meal. My brother became a gourmet cook himself when he began helping his wife in meal preparation. She declares that he left her behind. It was always fun to visit them and see what new concoction he had dreamed up. Rather than being intimidated by his involvement, his wife was quite happy to have him almost take over the meal preparation for guests.

Perhaps men often miss out because they feel that cooking and serving is just too mundane. Actually, there are few things that call for more creative powers than planning, shopping, cooking, and serving a meal in an attractive way. Isn't it strange that so many think cooking is a woman's work, when we all know that the most famous and world renowned chefs are men? The fact is, these days it is very difficult for a woman to break into this exclusive club. I know a girl who went to all the right schools to learn how to be a first-class baker. She was able to get several good jobs as a baker in good hotels in our area. Then she broke the barrier and was finally hired to be the chief baker at one of the city's finest hotels. She knew she could do it, but the five male chefs with whom she worked were sure she couldn't make it in their world. In fact, they saw to it that she didn't make it—they were very much intimidated by her deft fingers, the extra flourish she added to the exquisite pastries. They were convinced the field was theirs and did not appreciate a woman breaking through. No, cooking isn't just for women—it's as much for men.

It's a shame for us to get into a rut of thinking that only women can cook and entertain—or that a man would never want to. Many men love it. Even if it is just one particular dish he can prepare, it's his specialty. What a shame to deny men the joy of cooking and entertaining! We miss much by not urging them to give it a try. Don't knock it unless you've tried it! Wives, challenge your husband to get in there with you and see what fun it really is.

Perhaps we stumble over the idea of practicing hospitality for others' sakes, receiving nothing in return. Surely that is one facet, but it is not the whole gem. Is there anything wrong with entertaining for the pure joy and fun of doing it, not just looking at what it will produce? Many of us know how to give for the glory of God, but we haven't learned to receive that which is pure pleasure. This, too, can be to the glory of God.

I believe the potential is unlimited for bringing such rich blessing to God, to His family, to ourselves, and even to the world. None of us are super-saints, yet because we believe the Bible, we know that hospitality is one of the ministries commanded and encouraged. Probably we are most hung up on the fact that we just don't know how. If we didn't learn this gentle art as we grew up, there isn't a lot of help to get us started.

At a recent seminar on "Hallowed Hospitality," I discovered

that this is exactly the problem many Christians face: *how* to get started.

So let's begin by answering the question "Where should we begin?"

Chapter Two

Missing Out

The dreaded call came in the middle of the night. Through the crackle of the overseas connection, I understood enough to know that I must make the trip home to California. Mom was suffering from an inoperable brain tumor. Twenty-four hours later I boarded the Pan Am flight on a sticky June morning, leaving my husband and two little girls behind. Thiry-one hours later I arrived in San Francisco. The next morning Dad took me to the hospital and to my great delight and relief Mom recognized me. She had no idea why I was there and she was not to recognize me again. The tumor grew quickly and she slipped into a coma.

I spent each day at her side. She seemed to see me. Whenever I entered the room, the confused babble became clear. Something strange was happening. "Get the blue tablecloth and napkins from the cupboard," she said. "Put the good dishes on. Get the coffeepot on. There is cheese in the fridge, and fresh rolls in the breadbox. There is room for everyone at the table." Nothing confusing about those orders. Although the doctor called her state "semi-comatose," I was hearing what I had always heard as a young girl. There were obviously some nooks and crannies of her brain very much alive, where her thinking was quite clear. You see, the practice of gracious, unstinting hospitality had always been a part of her life as a pastor's wife. The rapidly growing tumor hadn't blotted out those memories yet. In fact, serving others, the recitation of Scripture and praying were the only areas of reality left in her mind. Nothing else made sense.

Through the hours at her bedside, my heart ached, yet as I thought about my life with my mom, some things were very clear. I found myself reaching back to childhood, to teenage years, to college years, and then to the years when she moved easily into the role of grandmother. She had held back nothing of herself—her encouragement, her enthusiasm, and her commitment to the cause of Christ—as my husband and daughter and I left for Pakistan to serve as missionaries on one of the most difficult fields of the world. When Dad and Mom had visited us in Pakistan six years before her illness, she had effortlessly joined with me in practicing hospitality from my own home.

Memory after memory came flooding in. I was struck with the fact that my whole life had been lived in an atmosphere of loving and caring, ministering and serving. Though Mom's brain was now slowly being squeezed to death by this ugly tumor, she couldn't escape from what her life had been. My own experiences as a missionary wife and mother began to line up with hers, and for the first time I began to grasp the depth and beauty of the heritage passed on to me.

All stories have an end. In two weeks she was ushered into the presence of the Savior she had served selflessly and faithfully for so many years. In my imagination's eye I can picture my mom in heaven, still serving. Am I off base as I visualize her still serving others in heaven in the gracious way she did here on earth? Though I don't pretend to understand much about what heaven will be like, I feel sure that if there is a banquet table, if afternoon coffee is served, Mom is functioning there as she did here.

In our contemporary church society we hear much about the need to restore the spirit of loving, of caring, of compassion, of serving; but we neglect one of the most beautiful and natural channels we have at our disposal. We talk much about spiritual gifts, but fail to realize that the gift of "helps" mentioned in Scripture is practiced most naturally in and through the home, in and through the art of hospitality. As we returned from 17 years as missionaries, we felt this lack. We needed someone to practice hospitality on us, to make the reentry a bit less traumatic.

We as a family have experienced the joy and excitement of keeping an "open home." Our ministry in Pakistan included heavy doses of hospitality and so does our life here. Throughout years on the mission field, we kept a guest book, though not always up-to-date. Sometimes when we pulled the book out people would groan. But the book is a record of those who passed through our home, ate at our table, slept in our beds, studied God's Word in our living room, prayed with us, and shared their burdens and heartaches with us. There were Americans, lots of them. But there were also representatives from almost every continent and many, many countries. There were all colors. They believed in many different creeds. They came from many religious persuasions. Most were a part of God's family, but not all. Most spoke English, but not all. I can't forget those who came with absolutely no knowledge of English. We smiled, laughed, gestured our way through many sticky situations.

What can I say about these people? Each one left behind a part of himself. They were not just isolated individuals who checked into our motel then left the next day. Each one brought a blessing we needed. Not all were easy to have. Some stayed too long. Many didn't stay long enough. But most left us better than we were when they came.

Non-Christians have also brought a special benefit. They have given us a clearer understanding of the importance of loving people even when they reject the message. They have given us a new burden for those who do not know Jesus Christ. It's great to know that we can leave encounters with non-Christians to God. Our responsibility is simply to provide a place where they can feel comfortable, a safe place where they feel sure that every encounter is not going to be a sermon. They need a place where they can be free from manipulation.

Let's expand upon the question we asked in chapter one: "If our home and our lives really are the most powerful combination for ministry, *and* if Scripture commands us to practice hospitality, then why do we neglect this important aspect of Christianity?"

I don't have the answer to that question. I can only begin to discover answers as I look at my own life. My theories come out of personal experience. One thing I know well is that I tend to be easy on myself. It is easy for any of us to make a habit of making excuses for not doing things we know we should do. By the same token we easily rattle off excuses for *doing* what we know we *shouldn't* do. Sometimes our excuses sound quite plausible—until we begin to pull them apart and look at them carefully. Most of the time our easily mouthed excuses hang by a flimsy thread. Just as those annoying cobwebs in the corner need to be brushed down in one fell swoop, so we need to knock down our feeble excuses for not using the powerful combination of our homes and our lives for ministry to a needy world. Once these defenses are knocked down, we can move on to begin to discover the joy and delight of being involved in this wonderful ministry of hospitality.

Let me help you discover what is keeping you from tasting the joy of using your own home for a unique ministry. At the outset listen to our story. Perhaps you are already thinking that hospitality is okay for us because we probably have all the modern conveniences that make entertaining easy, including a large bank account. Let me assure you, we don't.

Let me start with what we don't have. We don't have a deep freeze—the freezer part of our refrigerator is quite small. However, we don't look upon this as a detriment. It means we don't have to have a garden, and we don't have to spend all that time freezing what we have grown. We don't buy halves of beef with all that entails. We have enough room to keep all the ice cream we need, plus a few other odds and ends. That's what we're used to, so it really isn't a great sacrifice for us.

We don't have an electric dishwasher. There have been times when I have longed for one, but not very often. If I want guests to help in the kitchen, they almost always will. Much of the time I prefer to do the cleanup myself. Some of the time my husband helps. We manage quite nicely.

We don't have a microwave. We could probably afford one, but we're not yet convinced it would enhance our lives that much. At this point, it is something we can do without.

Our house is not large. We do have a small dining room, with a roomy built-in china closet. (In house-hunting, that was high on my priority list.) Our dining room table, which really seats eight, but we often have ten around it, nearly fills the room. I am sure we would still entertain if we had no dining room at all.

We don't have a family room. It would be nice to have one, but we get along quite well. A family room is surely an asset for informal entertaining, especially when children are involved, but it is not a necessity.

I'm sure we could use any one of these "have nots" as excuses for not practicing hospitality, but our family would definitely be the losers. You probably have your own built-in set of excuses, so perhaps this is the place to deal with reasonings that become hindrances to doing what we should.

"*I just don't know how.*" If that is really true and you really believe it, my advice would be simply, "Learn how." Perhaps you didn't learn the art of cooking as you were growing up. Maybe you came from a home where hospitality was not practiced. Then you will have to plunge in and learn. In many communities there are cooking classes available. There are literally hundreds of books available, even for beginners. Yet, learning hospitality really is no different from learning to drive an automobile. You can read all the books you like, but it is the behind-the-wheel experience that brings theory into reality.

A word to the men: If you are tempted to use the "I don't know how" excuse, there are wonderful books available for beginners. Go to your local bookstore and look at the shelves. You will be amazed at what is available. If you live alone in an apartment and want to invite just one other person to start with, find a basic cookbook such as *Better Homes and Gardens Cooking for Two*. Thumb through it and find the easiest page in the book. You will never learn how it's done until you give it a try. Start out simple, not too elaborate. You will be so proud of yourself when the meal has been cooked, served, and appreciated by you and your guest.

Or have you ever thought about asking your wife, your mother, or a special young lady to just give you the start you need by getting in there and helping you? Think how often we women have to ask for help. Any woman would be thrilled if a man asked for help in this area. Find someone you would trust to teach you, and get in there and learn how.

If you fall into this "I don't know how" category, avail yourself of all the helps available. Start in your supermarket. Swallow your pride and use mixes to begin with. They are tasty (some of them will be greatly enhanced by doctoring them a bit), nutritious, and most important, the instructions are written on the box or package. As you become more adept at cooking and entertaining, you will be able to adapt these mixes. To begin with, however, do exactly as the instructions say and you are almost always certain to win. I should also add that if you are a beginner, don't pay any attention to some experienced cooks who scoff at the use of mixes for anything. They can make you feel very guilty. Just don't be intimidated and do what you can. Keep in mind that even if you are serving a whole meal to guests, it need not be more than a packaged mix of some kind, a can of vegetables, a basket of store-bought rolls, a few sticks of celery, and a dish of ice cream. That's an adequate meal for anyone.

"I'm not a good cook." This excuse goes closely with the preceding one. Of course you will never know if you are a good cook unless you try. Add to this the fact that nobody begins by being a good cook. It is just like anything else—driving, swimming, playing an instrument—you have to start somewhere. You will find the more you do, the better and easier it becomes. It is also good to keep in mind that serving meals is not the only way of entertaining. There are thousands of other ways to practice the art of hospitality. Work at it. Find some way of using your own gifts, and you'll be surprised at what you can accomplish.

"My house isn't good enough or big enough." Not too long ago I overheard a conversation between the chairman of a Church Hospitality Committee and the woman she was trying to persuade to entertain guests on a given Sunday. The reply was, "Oh, no, I could never do that. My house just is not good enough. There is simply no way I could be involved like that." She sounded like she really meant it. I think she did. She missed the joy of sharing her home with others.

Recently I was discussing with two university students the subject of their outreach to non-Christians on their campus. Their faces lit up as they told me their strategy. They live in a huge dorm in the middle of the campus. They share one room and a tiny kitchen. They decided the little room was going to be the instrument for reaching out to non-Christians in that dorm. Every Friday night they invite guests in for dinner, usually just two at a time. They cook a meal on their small two-burner stove. It isn't fancy, and they have to eat it at their desks in the bedroom. They laughed as they told me about their fancy salad bowl. They scrub out their foot-square sink, put the plug in, and, *voila*, it becomes a good-sized salad bowl. It works fine. They are tasting the joy of the powerful combination for ministry— their home and their lives.

"I wouldn't know whom to ask." Now, that is a very strange excuse. We all know someone. You could begin by making a list of those who might be possible guinea pigs for your entertaining attempts. You could start with relatives, or neighbors, or church friends. I would suggest starting with someone you are going to feel comfortable with. Or perhaps you could find someone you know who has the same interests you have—perhaps another couple married about the same time you were. If you are a single adult, you could begin by asking someone else in your same situation. From this you can

move on to a group of people you want to reach—people you are sure you can minister to and who in turn will minister to you. If you are a woman at home alone during the day, why not start by just inviting a neighbor in for coffee and rolls? If you have children who play with other children whose parents you do not know, reach out by inviting them in for coffee or ice cream in the evening.

My husband and I had an experience recently which reminded us what can be done in gracious ministry through the home—even when there isn't a wife in that home. The wife in this case lay dying in the hospital. Her loving husband came to see her every night, usually bringing with him some homemade soup he had cooked up, some stew he had made himself—he actually brought many different things, all lovingly prepared with his own hands. We were so impressed with the joy and satisfaction he demonstrated through this sweet and loving ministry to his wife. One of the first things he did after she died was to invite us to his home for a dinner—just to thank us for what we had done for them both. As we stepped into his home for the first time, we knew that this man had a unique gift of making a house a home. The house was immaculate, tastefully decorated, the table was set beautifully, and the meal was a masterpiece of culinary experience. He was proudest of the pie he had made. As we left his home that evening, realizing that this gift was not something he had just learned but had obviously been the habit of his lifetime, we talked of what a ministry and witness he would be having through his home. The fact that his wife was no longer beside him was not going to stop him from allowing God to use his home.

There are many in our churches who are experiencing the pain and suffering that comes with the loss of a loved one. There aren't just widows but plenty of widowers as well. To both widows and widowers I would offer a strong challenge to let your home become your place of ministry. There is no better way to do this than through the practice of hospitality. It need not be elaborate—just something as a means of reaching out to others who are lonely and need a friend. One group of widows I know in a certain church get together once a week to play Trivial Pursuit. I'm sure they have all the cards memorized by now, but no matter. They take turns doing the entertaining and even include the widowers. Their own lives have become more satisfying, and they have the joy of knowing they are helping to meet the needs of the others as well.

"We really can't afford it." I am well aware that there are many

who really do have a hard time making ends meet. If you aren't careful, entertaining can put a heavy strain on an already stretched budget. Recently I was greatly encouraged by a woman who came to me after a meeting to tell me what God had been doing for their family in the preceding months. Her husband is in a ministry where they never are assured of a paycheck at the end of each month (they really know what it means to live by faith). As a family they had decided to commit themselves to the practice of Christian hospitality no matter how bare the cupboard or how low the bank account. With tears in her eyes she related story after story of how they had reached out to someone in need, not knowing how they would ever be able to put food on the table for themselves or their guests. Yet God had never failed them.

If you really can't afford to invite guests for a meal, then do something else. Hospitality is not just involved with meals—it can be doing anything for the person you invite. Hospitality is not just to be applied to a sumptuous and expensive meal. It has to do with caring, sharing, friendliness, and reaching out. That can be done just as well by sharing a cup of tea or coffee and a simple store-bought cookie. If that is absolutely all you can afford, then accept it. Thank God you can do that much, realizing that what is happening between you and your guests is more important than how much you spend.

I love the story of Mary and Martha and Lazarus found in the New Testament. Maybe the reason I like it so much is that I find a little bit of both Mary and Martha in me. I do love to become involved in the conversation before and after the meal (and if I have really gotten organized beforehand, it is possible to do this, even before the meal). On the other hand, I know there are many times when I am more like Martha. Do you ever wonder what Martha was fixing the day she entertained Jesus? It was perhaps nothing like we would serve for someone as important as Jesus, but I am sure that even in those days, she knew what was appropriate. Now, if they had had telephones in those days, can't you just imagine Jesus phoning ahead to say He was coming, making it very clear that He was coming to spend time with them? He didn't want anything elaborate. He just wanted to be with them. No doubt Martha, being the type she was, would get right into high gear. For Jesus it would have been enough just to be there with them, to sit with them, to tell them what was on His heart, to share His great truths with them. The very fact that they opened their home to Him was service enough. Surely Mary chose the better way—a cup of tea, a stool beside her Master, a time just to listen.

In the same way we must constantly remind ourselves that the ministry of hospitality has to do with caring, with sharing, with listening, with encouraging, with reaching out. Rather than being so wrapped up in demonstrating that we really do know how to cook an elaborate meal and serve it, we need to be concerned with the other aspect.

"I really don't have time." I would like to have a dime for every time I have used that excuse. Sometimes it really does have to do with an overcrowded schedule. I am well aware that for women who work full time, especially those who come home to a family with all kinds of needs, time is an important factor.

Nevertheless, for myself, I know full well that my neglect of hospitality often has to do with laziness. Frankly, I don't miss many meals myself, nor does my family. I work forty hours a week and am quite aware of the time I waste when not working.

Once we are convinced of the validity and the responsibilities of hospitality, we will make room for it. It need not be as often as once a week. You might like to set aside one evening a month, or one Sunday noon a month, when you are quite sure you can somehow pull it all together and entertain. Your circumstances will dictate how much you can do. But do something. To continually say, "I don't have time," is to rob ourselves of ministry to others and blessing to ourselves and our guests.

Here let me give a gentle but firm word of encouragment to husbands. So many wives these days work outside the home. I know from firsthand experience that the hours after work—between the arrival home and bedtime—are all too short to get the everyday things done. A wife does really have a lot of responsibilities, and a husband needs to get involved with his wife in the practice of hospitality. Remember, husbands are called to serve, too. That home is the husband's as well as the wife's. It is wonderful to be able to show the love of Jesus to those whom we invite. It is also wonderful to see a husband demonstrating the love of Jesus by sharing with his wife in the preparation, cooking, serving, and—yes—even the cleanup after guests have been entertained.

"I will have to wait until my children are grown." This is surely one of the saddest excuses we can use. As I look back to my own childhood, I realize that the "heritage of hospitality" was constantly

and unconsciously passed on to me. I remember a host of people who passed through our home, sat at our table, slept in our beds. I am thankful we children were very much involved in all that was going on. I have happy memories of helping set the table with the good dishes and the crystal. I loved to have the privilege of helping to wash things up and put them away. If you wait until your children are grown before you start practicing hospitality you will deny them an important lesson for their lives. Most of us don't like to deny our children anything, especially those things that are worthwhile. Hospitality—sharing what we have—is an aspect of the Christian life we need to be emphasizing and teaching all through their growing-up years. If they don't learn it at home, chances are they won't do much of it when they are grown. If they do learn it later, they will come to realize how much they missed.

I am aware that children need to be taught their place and also to be under control. I also realize with children present our entertaining necessarily will be much less formal than it is when they are gone. But they should be involved nevertheless. Help them to understand it is a very special privilege to have guests in their home. Remind them constantly that all the possessions you have come from the hand of a loving heavenly Father and that they are a gift to be shared with others. Help them see from the earliest age that sharing what we have been given is not just an option but a vital part of the teaching of Scripture.

Let me also add that there are times when children need to taste the experience of sitting down to a nicely set table with guests at hand, with tablecloth, good china, even crystal. They need to know that life isn't just place mats, plastic dishes, paper plates, or standing around in the kitchen munching on frozen pizza. You don't have to overdo on the more elegant entertaining, but your children surely should have a taste of it sometime. Don't wait until your children are grown. Teach them that the practice of Christian hospitality is a privilege, a delight, and a means of blessing to both guest and host.

"I don't have the right type of personality" or *"It makes me too nervous. It just isn't for me."*

Isn't it wonderful that we aren't all alike? Isn't it a blessing that we aren't all females—or males? Isn't it great that we aren't all Marthas—or Marys? God has gifted each one of us for some kind of service. Scripture seems to clearly teach that the Spirit has given *all* of us gifts. Romans 12 tells us that "we have different gifts, according to the grace given us. If a man's gift is prophesying, let him use it in proportion to his faith. If it is serving, let him serve; if it is teaching, let him teach; if it is encouraging, let him encourage; if it is contributing to the needs of others, let him give generously; if it is leadership, let him govern diligently; if it is showing mercy, let him do it cheerfully."

It is interesting that the gifts God had given for the purpose of making Christ's body work properly—serving, encouraging, and showing mercy—are not confined to women. Yet in our Christian circles today those gifts are pretty much left to the women to administer. When I think of serving, my mind and my heart goes to the picture of Jesus himself at the last supper going around to wash the feet of His disciples. What a disservice we do to the Body of Christ by relegating the gifts of service and encouragement and helps just to women. They are for all of us—there is no distinction. Even the gift of hospitality was never meant to be relegated to the women's corner. There are no special gifts for men and others for women. We are involved in ministry together—and this even includes hospitality.

Perhaps we have become so adept at mouthing feeble excuses because we have not developed a proper philosophy of Christian ministry through our homes. Hospitality is intrinsic to the Christian faith and to the Gospel itself. It is built right in and cannot be removed. For if I really believe that all I have has been given to me by a loving, caring God who delights in pouring His blessings on me, then it follows logically that what He has given out of His great heart of love is to be given back to Him in loving service to others. That is Christian servanthood, in which we experience the deep joy of serving and God gets the glory—a winning combination.

Hospitality is not only a fine art, a special gift, something we do. It is first and most importantly an attitude. Perhaps this is again part of the problem, part of the reason excuses flow so effortlessly from our lips. We get the cart before the horse—doing before we have tended to the *being*, the attitude. What is this attitude? First, developing the heart of a true servant. It begins when we realize that it really is more blessed to give than to receive, more blessed to serve than to be served. This, then, is the mysterious element that transforms the routine of getting organized, getting the house in order, serving a meal, and, yes, even the cleaning up, into an act of true worship to God. It transforms our service from a round of grudging activities and busyness to the production of results in our own lives as well as the lives of those we entertain. A true servant is one who is sensitive to the needs and wishes of the one he serves. The logical result is that we will be satisfied with what we have, happy to take what God has given us and use it for the good of others and for the glory of God.

Recently I heard an account of true servanthood. My friend's son is a pilot with Missionary Aviation Fellowship in Zaire. He flies people and supplies to remote mission stations often inaccessible by other means. Trips for delivering supplies, even for emergencies that without the plane would take days, are made in a matter of hours.

This son makes regular trips to a remote mission station in the jungle of Zaire, where for forty years a faithful missionary couple has ministered. The pilot radios ahead the time of his arrival. Then as he brings the plane down over the jungle for landing on the tiny airstrip he sees a little drama unfold beneath him. It happens every time. The missionary lady comes hurrying down the path to the airstrip with a basket, sometimes with an African helper carrying a folding table and a folding chair. As the pilot taxis to a stop, that lonely African airstrip is transformed into a dining room. The table is spread with a clean cloth. The basket is emptied of its contents: a place setting for one with a full meal. There he sits, in the heart of the African jungle, partaking of a meal lovingly and carefully served by God's special servants. After the meal, the table is cleared and folded up. The pilot climbs into the plane, says goodbye, and soon is on his way. As he dips his wings in a final farewell, even God's heart must be warmed. These dear servants of God used what He had provided to minister to the needs of another of His choice servants. They offered no excuses but simply, willingly used that powerful combination—their homes and their lives—to share and to serve. That poignant drama is enacted regularly, reminding them all of the sweetness and joy of a ministry of hospitality.

So we come full circle to where we began. "Our homes and our lives are indeed the most powerful combination for ministry to our world."

Dip in and begin to taste the sheer joy of Christian hospitality. What we do in this regard is truly significant in the total work of God. Most of us are not aware of our own potential in being true servants of God. Our greatest temptation is to seriously underestimate what Christ can do in us and the significance of what we do in and through our home in the total plan of God. What we do makes a significant contribution to God's work in this world. Jump in. Give it a whirl.

Chapter Three

Simple Beginnings

The intense heat had already settled on the city that morning as we drove to the outskirts. Our Volkswagen Bug carried not only our family of four—parents and two little girls—but the man who served as our "mali" (gardener) for the past ten years. He was a little man, sad-faced and burdened. He had every reason to be sad-faced. With some fat on his bones, he wouldn't have looked so tiny. As it was, I doubt if he weighed ninety pounds. We didn't need a full-time mali. In fact, we didn't even need a part-time mali. This little man had come to our door with such a tale of suffering and grinding poverty that we would have hired him no matter what. He had a wife and four children and another child on the way. We had helped them through times of sickness, disaster, and destitution. His wife had taken the clothing I gave her and used every part of it for her children, showing her skills at sewing. She had been in and out of the hospital with T.B. Their little girl had rheumatic fever, which had left her terribly debilitated. Yet with all the help we gave them, we always felt we were barely scratching the surface of their needs.

Most recently this man had suffered a severe case of shingles. But now he was on his feet again. His gratefulness was almost embarrassing. It wasn't enough to say it in words. He had the habit of falling on his face, clasping our feet, and pouring out his thanks. He told us over and over again that "Allah" (the Muslim name for God) had sent us to keep his family from dying.

He was a devout Muslim. He often told us that the difference in our religions made our expressions of love and care to him even more poignant. As his ultimate expression of gratitude to us, he had invited us to his house for morning tea. It was no good to try to argue with him. It was clearly what he had to do, and it was also what we had to do. As we all bounced along in the car, I kept looking at him with his sad face, saying to myself, "This is no good. They shouldn't be spending money to entertain us. That money needs to be used to feed their children." I have since learned that that is a very Western way of reasoning. It is not always the right way. To deny his family the right and religious privilege of entertaining us would have been the height of callousness and insensitivity on our part.

We arrived at his little village just outside the city. The streets became narrower, the houses all squashed together. Soon we were bumping along a road barely wide enough for the car. The heat trembled between the mud walls, and the dust swirled, flies swarming everywhere. Mingled with the smell of dust was the smell of open drains, animals, and fires fueled by cow-dung patties. Finally we came into a little clearing. As he jumped out of the car, he beamed, bowed low, and said, "This is my home. You are welcome." Yes, this was home and he displayed it with pride—a tiny hovel with floor of polished mud. The walls were made from scraps of tin, burlap, and cardboard which had obviously been scavenged from garbage heaps here and there. Two little rooms adjoined the open courtyard. In one corner of the courtyard was the kitchen. The stove was a hole in the ground stoked with cow-dung patties on which a little kettle was boiling. The children peeked from behind a partition made of scraps of cardboard. I spotted a little table in the corner. On the table were a faded cloth and places for four—cup, saucer, and spoon. Muslims don't usually sit down with their guests. They prefer to hover around ready to serve them.

As his wife poured the tea into the cracked cups, we began the job of swishing the flies off the small plate of biscuits set before us. There in that hovel we dined like kings and queens. They offered us the best they had, doing it willingly, joyfully, and without holding back anything. They were convinced that no excuse would be good enough to keep them from expressing their thanks to us in this way. It wasn't much, but it was all they had. We soaked up the love and gratitude of this family. They reminded us in their own way that hospitality can indeed be blessed and hallowed, no matter what the circumstances. I did a lot of soul-searching on the way home. I know that I have never been the same since that experience.

What about you? What most often keeps you from practicing hospitality? What excuses do you find yourself using most often for not practicing hospitality?

So many make the statement: "I know I should, but I never have. I'm scared to death. Please tell me how I can begin." Along with those statements come the excuses that sound something like this: "We don't have much money," "I'm not a very good cook," "My kids behave so badly."

That family in Pakistan practiced hospitality within their own means and culture, refusing to fall back on all the good excuses they could have used. That is all that is asked of us, too. If I had any advice to Christians wanting to embark on the course of using their homes in a ministry of hospitality, I would say, "Start where you are." Don't use the excuse that you will wait until you get into a bigger house, until you have a better kitchen. You have to begin somewhere and sometime. Start now, right where you are.

Let me say a word here about all the beautiful magazines on the newstands. I enjoy them, but I do have to be careful. They show pictures of unbelievably beautiful homes, incredibly elegant table settings, and fantastically scrumptious-looking foods. My friends, if you think you should wait until you can entertain like that, you'll never get started. I am not advocating that you not look at those magazines. They are wonderful for ideas. Just remember, they are not the standard by which you can entertain. They are nothing but a valuable resource for you, so let them be that and no more. Remember also that most of those pictures come from test kitchens. If the photograph is from someone's home, a decorator or specialist has fixed it so it's just right. If these magazines make you dissatisfied, it's probably best to leave them alone. Read them, enjoy them, and then forget them.

Here are a few more suggestions for beginners:

Start simply. For your first foray into the world of entertaining, don't think you have to invite your whole Sunday school class at once. Start simply, perhaps with one couple, or even one person. Choose an easy menu and give it a whirl.

Be yourself. Decide what you are most comfortable with—sit-down dinners, barbecues, coffee parties, buffets, teas, after-church functions, breakfasts, or brunches. Find some means of entertaining you enjoy and where you can be yourself. Don't pretend.

Don't overdo. Don't bite off more than you can chew. (This is one of my biggest problems. I tend to overdo almost everything. I'm still learning.) You have to learn how to begin, but you also have to learn when to quit. This applies to the number of people, to the type of menu, to conversation, and to ending the occasion.

Know how to pace yourself. This is the art of knowing when enough is enough. If you can't entertain people twice a week, don't. If once a month is all you can do, then stop there. You also need to learn to stop even when hosts say, "Oh, don't go home yet," when you know it is past time. Usually it is simply being sensitive to the needs and feelings of others.

Be creative. Don't make what other people do your model. Find out what you can do best and do it—and become famous for it! Yes, the ego is involved in all of this.

To those quick suggestions for beginners I add a few "for instances":

If you have young children, you could invite another family with children about the same age to come for a barbecue. Of course, weather and your backyard situation will dictate this. When children are involved, it is often easier to function outside where things are naturally more informal. However, even with outside barbecues or outside dinners (they don't have to be cooked outside, you know—you can cook inside and carry the whole dinner outside with no trouble at all), you need to get organized ahead of time. Can't you remember barbecues that were near disasters because the host had not reckoned with the time it takes to get coals going? Sam and I roar with laughter remembering a night at a friend's home. Not only had the husband not planned for the time it takes to get the coals going, but for some reason the coals stubbornly refused to burn. We waited and waited and waited. The host got more and more angry and his wife talked faster and faster. All in all, it was a very long evening, becoming more and more tense as the minutes ticked by. If you aren't used to working with coals outdoors, it's probably not wise to practice on your guests.

I don't have a lot of patience with grilling meat outside. I personally prefer to plan a nice meal that can be cooked in the oven and carried outside at the right moment. Surely one of the plusses for this method is that the children can be playing outside while the meal is being cooked. For this kind of entertaining I wouldn't think of using anything but paper plates. Make it as easy as possible.

Of course there are other easy ways to serve. My mother did a great deal of entertaining after church on Sunday nights. She wasn't a beginner by any means, but for one who doesn't have a lot of experience, Sunday evenings are an easy way to begin. You can seat guests around the table, or serve from the coffee table. The menu can be very simple—a snack and something to drink. That way you avoid the pressure of preparing a whole meal as well as giving the host or hostess the opportunity of sitting down and visiting in this relaxed type of entertaining.

During my first year of seminary I lived with two elderly ladies. To this day when I think of after-church entertaining, I remember the lovely table they set. They usually had cold sliced meat left from Sunday dinner, bread and cheese, pickles, sometimes Jell-o salad or fruit sauce and a cookie for dessert. I could hardly wait to get home from church to see what was on the table for me.

We have a number of friends who do almost all of their entertaining in this way. They feel it's what they do best. It's inexpensive and not too demanding for those who work away from home. I shouldn't fail to mention that cleanup is easier in this situation.

If it's your kids you worry about, remember the kids are usually pretty keyed-up after church. I suspect they will want something to eat when they get home anyway. Actually, it is easier to control kids for a shorter period of time like this. Give it a try.

Begin simply. This applies to all kinds of entertaining. If you have people for a whole meal, make it a simple one. Serve it simply. Don't jump in too deep at the beginning. Feel your way along and experiment. Discover for yourself how to make the whole process of practicing hospitality enjoyable for you and your guests. If you're having a barbecue, you really don't have to have anything more than hamburgers and fixings, perhaps a salad or baked beans, and a dessert. There's nothing wrong with a bowl of fruit for dessert.

For an inside meal you can prepare a simple, inexpensive casserole, some kind of bread, a salad or vegetable, and dessert and drinks. I suggest you do a little experiment. Go to your cupboards and refrigerator right now and try to come up with a menu for a nice, simple meal you wouldn't mind serving to guests, using *only* what is already there. With a little imagination, you would be surprised what a nice meal you could fix.

I know from experience that it can be difficult to be yourself when you're all hot and bothered about entertaining guests. Even when you try to relax, you find your stomach getting tied up in knots. I don't know how to tell you to be yourself. I have a hard time convincing myself that I don't have to try to act like someone else. But I keep working at doing what is right and proper for me. I know what I am trying to accomplish—I know my own hang-ups, I know my own strengths and weaknesses. Don't try to duplicate what someone else is doing. Just learn to do your own thing.

And guard against the tendency to overdo. It's too easy to spend more than you can afford, cook more than is necessary, fret more than is wise, or fuss more than you or your family can stand. There is the huge temptation to make a big deal out of something that isn't a big deal. Another way to say it is this: *Don't take yourself too seriously.* Learn to laugh at yourself. Learn to have fun with it.

Here's what I mean. If you can't comfortably seat twelve people for a sit-down dinner, then don't invite that many. If it's bedlam at your house when there are two extra children at the table, then plan something for later in the evening when the kids are in bed. If your backyard is a disaster, then don't plan something for the backyard. If you don't have a dining room, then use your coffee table, or plan a buffet dinner.

On the same subject of overdoing, another word of caution. Don't get so wrapped up in hospitality that you never leave time for you and your family to be alone. Face it, there are times when you need to be alone. There are times when you just don't feel up to having guests. Don't worry or feel guilty about it. Do just as much as you can do—pull back or quit for a while when you can't handle any more.

Can't you remember evenings with friends that were nearly ruined because someone didn't have sense enough to quit? Boredom and exhaustion are two ever-present problems. Sometimes as host and hostess we have to help our guests along. Sometimes we almost have to help them out of the house! Cranky children can be a sign that things have gone on long enough. Do something to bring it to an end. It's better to quit while people are still having fun and enjoying themselves than to go on too long.

We have a very dear friend who has developed evening-ending to a fine art. I have never known anyone else who does it with such grace. I wouldn't dare to try it. Quietly, sweetly, yet firmly, he announces that it is getting late. He rationally reminds us that we all have busy days tomorrow (even if we don't). He prays, and that's it. What can you do? You head for the door. I have nothing but admiration for the gentle way he can bring an occasion to an end. He always gets away with it.

Then I have a lot of admiration for people who dare to be different. I like a "free spirit" in the area of entertaining. This has nothing to do with going beyond the bounds of propriety. Each of us ought to be exploring every possibility for being creative in our entertaining. I used to think that when I invited someone to my home for a meal, I had to have meat, potatoes, gravy, salad, two vegetables, rolls, pickles, dessert and drink. That's nonsense. I am thankful that I am no longer in that rut. After all, how many ways can you fix a roast? Not many. I have a cupboard full of cookbooks and notebooks filled with recipes I have collected. Those cookbooks and recipes need to be used.

One of my favorite challenges is to take a basic recipe and change it. Much of our entertaining these days is with college students, who make great guinea pigs, and so I do a lot of experimenting on them. Actually, it's a bit of a joke. They taste the concoction and then the questions begin: "What is this? What's this called? Where did you get the recipe?" I'm good at hemming and hawing and beating around the bush. It's usually something I never tried before. The moment of truth usually comes when they ask for the recipe. Sometimes they like to give a name to some nameless concoction. Something like "Gracie's Beefy Noodle Bake." Or, "Gracie's Crunchy Yummy Spicy Bake." Or, "Gracie's You-Name-It Mystery Dish." Names aren't important—being creative is. I like to stand in front of the cupboard, survey what is there, and then use my imagination to concoct ways to use what I have. It might be living dangerously, and it's probably not too wise for beginners, but it surely is fun.

Don't be afraid to use mixes from the supermarket. I look upon these as the basic ingredient, and from there I take off. Many of the mixes have suggestions for variety, but don't stop with those. For instance, almost anything can be enhanced by onion soup mix or cheese soup mix. Nuts, raisins, pineapple, or grated carrots can be added to any cake to make something unusual. You might even make guests think what you are serving is from scratch. I remember the evening my aunt and uncle ate with us. He consumed biscuits and more biscuits. Finally he looked me in the eye and said, "Will you give my wife the recipe for these?" I got up and brought the wrapper from a tin of Hungry Jack biscuits. He was amazed and I was delighted. Let your pride down a bit and begin by using all the help you can find on supermarket shelves. When you have more experience, more time, more patience, and more courage, you can tackle the "from scratch" concoctions.

In conclusion, don't be too staid about your mission of practicing hospitality. Chances are that you will never serve dinner to the President and First Lady. So don't take yourself too seriously. You might as well have fun. Laugh at yourself when the meal is over and you suddenly remember the salad is waiting in the refrigerator. Smile at yourself when you let the rolls stay in the oven a bit too long. In one casserole I served to college kids there were little nut-like creatures. Someone asked if I put nuts in it. "No, not exactly," I replied. Then I had to confess that the nut-like creatures were actually dried-up pieces of macaroni that hadn't gotten soaked in the sauce. I broke them off and stirred them into the casserole. They really did taste like nuts. We all had a good laugh.

Have fun—be yourself, be creative, don't overdo, know when to stop, start simply. But most importantly, *get started*.

Chapter Four

A Tale of Two Mothers

In America we loudly extol the rich heritage of our mothers. Actually, this is true in most cultures of the world. Mothers are always something special. We talk about motherhood as being one of those rock-like aspects of our heritage that cannot and must not be destroyed. I heartily agree.

Most people consider themselves richly blessed if they point to one godly mother who had a part in shaping and molding their lives. I am doubly blessed—I can point to two mothers whose faith, deep commitment to the cause of Jesus Christ, and servant-like lifestyles have had a part in making me what I am.

My own mother has been called by many of her friends the ideal preacher's wife. In her were combined the Christlike assets of humility, service, hard work, and love for people, especially those who were in distress and hurting. She stood like a rock beside my father in his long years of ministry—always loyal to her husband, and most important, totally committed to serving Christ through her home. My happy memories of those growing-up years are of a mom who was firm but gentle, who was serious about her own Christian life, and who tirelessly served Christ through her service to others.

My memories are of sounds, smells, sights, touches, all bound up in the life of a tiny woman who brought four strapping children into the world. We lived humbly and frugally, but I never remember her longing for what other people had or being what other people seemed to be. She was a bundle of energy, a creative thinker, with a delightful sense of humor. Most important, as she served her Master,

39

she did it with her own inimitable style. She was able to take the gifts God had given her and totally be herself. And it was only after God had called her home that we fully realized how indispensible she was to my father's ministry and life.

After four miserable years alone, my father returned to a small town in Minnesota to rediscover a lovely widow who, with her family, had been my parents' closest friend in their ministry there. My husband and I were missionaries in Pakistan when this romance began to bud, a story we loved to urge Dad to tell. His eyes would twinkle as he told of the long distance phone calls, the letters (some of which she even shared with us), and the final culmination of a wedding in a little church in southwestern Minnesota. He was 82 and she was 72. Both our families were thrilled. We knew they needed each other. She was extremely intelligent, a hard worker, and one we were sure would take good care of our dad.

I am not comparing these two ladies. They don't need to be compared. They had some things in common. They were hard workers, totally committed to Christ and my dad's Christian ministry, and they both were the personification of real spiritual humility. But each of those elegant ladies brought to their marriage relationships a distinct and unique style, a special personality, a creative way of ministering through the home. And most amazingly, they both became to me the very epitome of what a Christian home should be: a special combination of heritage, physical strength, emotional makeup, family background, and deep spiritual insight.

These two ladies beautifully illustrate that the practice of Christian hospitality must begin in the heart and then be carried out in a manner that is strictly "you." Webster defines hospitality as "the welcome of guests with warmth and generosity." I would add to that definition, "and with a peculiar and unique style."

Both the Old and New Testaments indicate that among the patriarchs, the "welcome of guests with warmth and generosity" was not just cultural, but a response of their daily lives lived in the presence of the living God. This is also true in the life of the early church. The epistles make it very clear, as do the teachings of Jesus himself, that the entertainment of guests has always been a natural outgrowth of our relationship to Jesus Christ—it is intrinsic to what we believe.

Christian hospitality has to do first of all with attitude. While hospitality is, at its core, more concerned with being than doing, it is also bound up in who we are as individuals. Each of us, endowed with the Holy Spirit of God, lives in this world as a distinct individual. We are all Christians, yet have different lifestyles, personalities, and family relationships. In the same way we perform hospitality in thousands of different ways.

You no doubt have already made hospitality a distinct part of your lifestyle. If so, you have found the more you do, the easier it has become. Also, the way you put it into practice cannot be dictated by what the magazines say and show you, what the recipe books say, or by what others think you should do. Only you can decide what means of Christian hospitality you are going to use. You don't need to look at other people for your example. You can decide what is best for you and your family, depending on where you live, how much time and money you have, and how much your body and nervous system can take.

This realization should "free us up" to be ourselves. We are not all locked into the same mold. There are no fancy gimmicks we need to make the welcome of our guests a heart-warming experience. Generosity is practiced in a myriad of ways. There are no special formulas. We can experiment and then decide what is best for us.

In other words, I must find what is "me" or "us" or that which is most natural and enjoyable for me. Along with all the recipes, the entertaining tips, the guest lists, we must be ourselves. For some of us, it is a long process of learning to be natural. When we have achieved this, we will find joy and deep satisfaction in what we do for others through our homes.

Use this chapter to find the method that most easily fits your lifestyle. I can't begin to touch on all the ideas I've gathered for years and have only begun to use. The exciting thing is that we can each be as creative as we dare to be. Perhaps some of these ideas will strike fire with you. Don't be afraid to try different styles. If it doesn't work or seem right for you, find something else. As you consider each of these ways of entertaining, keep in mind that they have come from someone else. God has gifted you, given you creative powers. He knows everything about your personality, your budget, what kind of home you have, even your family. He will be honored when you use for His glory what He has entrusted to you.

Just keep in mind as we fly through these ideas that all through the Bible God reminds us that He can take the simplest, most down-to-earth happening in a life and surround it with a holy aura. He can lift it from the commonplace and everyday, and expand it into something beautiful and God-honoring. He can do the same with us and our entertaining.

Dessert. This is a great way to begin, as well as being very economical. Why not decide right now that before the week is out, you will give someone a call and ask that person to come over for a dish of ice cream—after church, after a meeting, or just during the early evening hours? It doesn't require much time, much preparation, or much money—just a dish of ice cream, a cookie and a cup of tea or coffee. It's as simple as that. Of course the purpose is not primarily eating, but fellowship. It can be very satisfying.

Here's one that never fails to produce exclamations from my guests. In the summertime, I like to use my heavy glass sundae dishes which I picked up at a good sale. You can get by with a pint of sherbet—two different kinds if you prefer—and several kinds of fruit. In the bottom of each sundae dish, put a small ball of sherbet, followed by a tablespoonful of crushed pineapple, another ball of sherbet, a spoonful of frozen or fresh strawberries, another ball of sherbet, and top it all with a few banana slices and a dollop of Dream Whip, maybe even a cherry on top. The thick glass of the dishes makes it look like you are serving large portions, but actually you have gotten by with very little sherbet and just small portions of fruit. Use your iced tea spoons, set them on a tray and carry them to the guests. They'll love it. Remember, don't get in a rut and invite the same guests all the time. Use it as a means of getting acquainted with new people.

After-church entertaining. Unfortunately these days many churches don't have evening services. I have already written about some of my happy memories of after-church spreads by my mother and others. My parents didn't always plan ahead whom to invite. There were times when I watched my father, sitting straight and proper in his pulpit chair during the song service, write a note and send it down to my mother. No one else knew what it was, but we knew Dad had sent a note suggesting someone to invite.

For food, the sky is the limit—sloppy joes, pizza, or just rolls and different kinds of spreads, with potato chips or other salties on the side. With a cup of coffee or tea, there is something warming and peaceful about ending God's special day around the table with friends.

Sunday dinners. At this stage of our lives, we are finding Sunday dinners fast becoming our specialty. I love the challenge of getting things ready ahead of time. I believe that much of the deep joy I experience in preparing Sunday meals for guests has to do with my childhood. It can be carried out only by planning ahead. But it's wonderful.

Breakfasts and brunches. The world is full of people who are "nonbreakfast" people, even though the best medical authorities tell us breakfast is very important. There are also many who are just not "morning people." If you fit into that category, you might consider a brunch a more viable option than serving breakfast. If you are a working family, breakfasts and brunches will have to be done on Saturday or Sunday, but that isn't all bad either. I think it's a wonderful idea. I have heard of one homemaker who finds that Sunday morning breakfast is an ideal time to entertain. It has its own built-in time limits, it can be very simple (fresh rolls, fruit juice, and coffee), and it takes minimum preparation. If you are not a morning person, you will probably think this idea is insane. But it really isn't. I happen to be a breakfast-lover, but my husband isn't, so it's hard for me to sell him on this kind of entertaining.

For a Saturday brunch, you would probably want to have something more substantial. How about trying a lovely "cheese strata," which can be prepared the night before and baked to be ready just when the guests come? Add several slices of bacon, a fruit cup, a sweet roll or piece of toast, and a pot of steaming coffee. For a special touch, serve a cantaloupe boat with a tiny scoop of sherbet, topped with a colorful little paper Japanese umbrella. It looks beautiful. If you have a patio or veranda, breakfast outside is special as you enjoy the fresh morning beauty.

Sunday afternoon "high tea." During our years in Pakistan, we worked closely with God's special servants from England, New Zealand and Australia. The British "high tea" held a special fascination for me. Since supper in the British Empire is served much later than it is in the U.S., they often have "high teas" in the late afternoons. Serve tiny sandwiches (ever hear of the famous British cucumber sandwiches?), relishes, cheeses, crackers, sliced meat, fruit cups—whatever suits your fancy. "High tea" is best served from a coffee table, or even better, from a tea cart. If you don't have either, use any table you have.

Barbecues and outdoor entertaining. Entertaining outside automatically produces an atmosphere of informality. For those of us who live in Minnesota, we probably can't do too much of this. Weather is a limitation, of course, but so is the mosquito menace. We dare not delay too long in getting started with our outdoor entertaining because the season will be over before we know it. Backyard (or side yard or even front yard) entertaining need not be complicated or lavish. It need not even include a grill and all the preparation that entails. There is no rule against preparing a meal indoors in the oven. We often do this. When it's all ready, we simply carry it out. In many ways it is easier. The important thing is not so much what you eat, or even how it is prepared, but who you shared it with. Make use of the good things available only in the summer, such as fresh corn on the cob, fresh strawberries, and garden vegetables. The point of it all is the fellowship we enjoy by partaking of the good things God has given us.

Share a picnic. Again, in Minnesota, our picnic season is very short, but how we enjoy the little time we have! It's fun to call a friend and say, "Meet us at the park—just bring yourselves; we're bringing the food." Many people love picnics but hate the preparation involved—packing the picnic basket especially—and detest even more putting things away when they get home. Well, I don't. My children gave me a lovely picnic basket recently, and I love packing it up and hauling it off to the park. Actually, I find myself looking longingly at that basket all winter long, and the anticipation helps keep me going through the long winters. We need to learn from the Europeans, who have developed the fine art of having simple spur-of-the-moment picnics. A loaf of bread, a block of cheese, a few slices of meat, some fresh fruit and something to drink, and off to the park for a picnic. It is effortless, and a wonderful way to share a meal with friends.

Game nights. With all the popular Trivia games, game nights seem to have come back into vogue. I am simply amazed at the people who tell me that they stayed up until all hours playing games with their friends. I am thankful we are back to this. For so many years, the television annihilated these fun evenings. Perhaps we have moved on a bit and come to the realization that the ugly square box, besides having very few redeeming factors of its own, was a poor substitute for close fellowship and fun we can have as we play games. It isn't difficult anymore to get a few people together for an evening of games. Even the old faithful games have not been forgotten—like Dutch Blitz, Monopoly, Rook, or countless others. Just recently I was told by one of the Senior Citizens in my church that she gets together quite regularly with three other widows to play Scrabble.

Since we are concerned not so much with the games themselves but with the hospitality, we need to think of what refreshments we can offer these avid game players who come to share our homes. Again, refreshments need not and probably should not be fancy or elaborate. They can be as simple as popcorn and fruit, or something that may take more time like pizzas or sloppy joes. If you know your guests well, you may even ask them to each bring something to munch on while the games are going on. Then the responsibility isn't all yours. The responsibility is yours, however, to see that the occasion moves along smoothly. There are those who simply must win every game, or who take so long at their turn that everyone else is bored (especially in Trivia), who simply must blurt out the answer even though it isn't their turn. You might even find there are people in the group who simply don't like to play games at all. Don't make them. Some people just like to sit and watch. Make the evenings relaxing and fun for everyone.

Morning or afternoon coffee times. Recently a student from my husband's Evangelism class told us about his girlfriend. She is deeply burdened for her neighbors. She decided that the one day a week when she doesn't have to go to work, she will go door-to-door, inviting her neighbors in for a cup of coffee and a homemade roll. She will begin with simple hospitality, a time of visiting around the table, a time to get acquainted, and then just see what God will do with these efforts. She wants her little home to be available and open at all times. Her dream is that eventually she will be able to get these ladies involved in a Bible study. These earnest efforts on her part may do that, but whatever the end result, this young lady wants her home to be used for the glory of God through Christian hospitality. I am sure He will richly bless her efforts.

Parties and potlucks. I don't pretend to know much about the art of giving parties. I am not even sure I can say that I enjoy parties. I much prefer quiet evenings with friends, new and old, in an unstructured atmosphere. There are many people who love nothing more than a good party. If you are one of those, go for it. There are many helps at your disposal and I have nothing but admiration for those who can come up with new and creative ideas for giving parties. For those who are really interested in developing this special mode of entertaining, one of the best helps you can find is the book *Creative Hospitality* by Marlene LeFever. It isn't just another party book, but one that outlines in great detail steps to be taken to accomplish the specific goal for each occasion. She includes menus, games, invitations—almost every detail for hosting a good party, one that will glorify God and bring people together.

Soup suppers. The popularity of soup and salad bars in restaurants has made us aware again of the versatility and appeal of soup. Do you enjoy making soup? Do you relegate a menu of soup to those times when your family is alone? I think most of us do. Has your mother passed on to you any soup recipes you know are tasty, nutritious, and sure to bring rave reviews? Why not try them on guests? We have a friend who ought to write a book on the fine points of making soup. She is famous for her soups. She has done it enough that she knows how to plan ahead and serve the meal with a minimum of fuss and bother. Her husband is a college professor and she uses her famous soups as the medium of entertaining and getting acquainted with her husband's students. Once a week, they invite a number of his students to their home for a soup supper. She sets the time at 5:30 and makes it clear that they are free to leave to get back to their studying after supper. She has entertained hundreds of students, treating them to her delicious soups, a welcome change from cafeteria food. Most importantly, their soup suppers have afforded her and her husband an opportunity to get to know these budding young scholars in a more intimate atmosphere. Preparation time is minimal, serving time is short, and everyone is satisfied.

I could mention many more of these styles of entertaining. The point is not so much what you do, but that you do something. Chances are you have already found your own particular style. If so, develop it for God's glory.

But what about those who for one good reason or another simply cannot invite people into their homes? We don't want them to miss out on the blessing that comes from sharing. There are ways to get involved in hospitality apart from what you can do in your home. And as you develop an attitude of giving and sharing and caring, you will find the same blessings of God showered upon you as those who are able to use their homes.

For one thing, it is always fun and rewarding to make things in your own kitchen and carry them to others. In small towns at least, this is done at times of sickness or death, but it surely isn't limited to those times. Sometime just bake a pan of rolls and take them to a friend or neighbor—just for the joy of it. We love to do this with our neighbors. Near to our house lives a man all by himself. He is healthy and able to fend for himself, but he's all alone. We have invited him to our home many times, but for some reason he finds it hard to accept our invitations. So we keep sending things over for him. He has never refused anything we have taken to him, and we know he is very grateful. I would rather he would come and share meals with us, but until he can do that, we just keep sending the goodies over to him.

We should also do the same when there are new people in the neighborhood or in the church. A pan of rolls, a plate of cookies, a loaf of bread—it isn't what we take that is important. The crux of the matter is, we are reaching out to that person with our own special creation, thereby communicating to him that we are aware of his presence, that we care, and that we want to be his friend. I have never met anyone yet who can refuse these gifts of love.

If you really cannot entertain from your home (perhaps there is a member of the family who simply will not tolerate guests in the home—such things do happen), it is almost always possible to give financial help to those who can. We had such a lady in our ministry in Pakistan. She was a wonderful Christian, but her husband could not stand Christians, especially missionaries. She was not allowed to entertain in her home, although she wanted to so badly. She would often come to me after a church service and hand me a 20-rupee note and whisper, "Here, use this to help entertain your guests." I have no doubt that God accepted her gift and was pleased.

If we are involved in our churches at all, there are also many ways to be involved in hospitality in God's house, if not our own. My suggestion is that as we get involved in serving meals, planning special functions in our churches, we are involved in Christian hospitality.

Let me appeal to your egos a bit. Are you famous for anything? Do you feel there is one thing that makes you stand out from the ordinary where the preparation of food is concerned? Let me illustrate. My mother-in-law in her little Missouri town was famous for her apple dumplings. One taste of them made it very clear why. When a church dinner was scheduled, there were actually church members, usually men, who would call her to ask if she was going to bring her apple dumplings. If the answer was in the affirmative, you can be sure they were there, first in line, since they knew full well that there would be only 16 servings of dumplings. She got a tremendous sense of satisfaction and joy out of her famous apple dumplings.

My own mother was well known for her Swedish meatballs. She knew beyond the shadow of a doubt that people were going to rave about them. She didn't even try to be humble about it—she knew they were good and so did everyone else. I especially remember one seven-foot-male friend who, when invited to our house, asked for them. My mother always knew she needed to at least triple the recipe when he came. He attacked them like a giant suction machine. She loved it!

Do you know any men who have a specialty? I do. People who make good fudge are very special in my book. The best fudge I know is made and delivered by a friend, the dean of a college. He knows he has mastered the art of fudge-making, and I think he gets just as much enjoyment and fun out of giving it away as the recipients get from eating it.

Another friend is a real pro at making Chinese food. He got started by reading an article in the newspaper that challenged him. He went out and bought a wok and now is well known for his delicious Chinese dishes. Do you think he doesn't get a big kick out of all the oohing and aahing that comes from his guests as they eat his masterpieces? Of course he does—he loves it.

So don't worry about giving into your ego a bit. Find what suits you best, what is easiest and most efficient for you and what gives you the most satisfaction. Develop it and embellish it. Work on it, refine it. Fine tune it. Soon it will become an extension of your own creative lifestyle and personality. Use the creative gifts God has given you and see what happens. Try new things—don't get stuck in a rut—and by all means don't let anyone else set the pace for you. Learn to be yourself, to be natural and relaxed, to be comfortable in your own little niche. Bask in the glow that comes from doing your own thing well. Let God take the gifts that He has bestowed and use them in a unique way within your own circle of friends. The result will be blessing for others, unspeakable joy for you, and glory to God.

Remember that hallowed hospitality has first to do with attitude. It has more to do with being than doing. It requires first of all a deep love for God, a determination to be obedient, a commitment to true servanthood, and a love for people.

Chapter Five

Hot-House Christians

It took us a long, long time to accept an invitation to a cocktail party. "What?" you ask. "A real live, decadant cocktail party? I thought you were missionaries!" This is not the place to go into a lengthy discussion of the pros and cons of accepting such an invitation. It took us a long time. The friendship of missionaries is not exactly sought after and cultivated by the diplomatic and business communities of large foreign cities. Sometimes, for various reasons, an acquaintance may feel it would be expedient to include missionaries in the guest list. We haven't been to many cocktail parties, but to enough to have learned that they are a very strange social custom. People who go all the time classify them as "boring," "artificial," "a complete waste of time." They often are. People stand around with a glass in their hand, looking proper and sophisticated. Snatches of mindless conversation, loud uncomfortable laughing, shuffling around—all the time eyes darting here and there trying to spot another group that looks more interesting, more stimulating. Really, they are pitiful and never humorous.

So why am I talking about cocktail parties in a book about hospitality? Many Christians are the hot-house variety. Get us out of our own environment, where we are confident and secure, and we absolutely fall apart. I was that way. Even though my home was the epitome of gracious Christian hospitality extended to all people and practiced on every level, I scarcely remember having non-Christian people in our home on a strictly social level. I don't mean to condemn anyone for that. Maybe there were more than I can remember. That's beside the point. But here's where the cocktail party comes in. The fact of the matter is, a lot of us Christians simply do not know how to relate on a social level with people who are outside the family of Jesus Christ. I was that way and that's why the acceptance of a cocktail party invitation was such a traumatic experience. We accepted only because the occasion was a farewell for dear friends—in other words, we felt an obligation to go for the sake of our departing friends. For one thing, we were aware that government and business people didn't have a very high view of missionaries. So who wants to go where they will be looked down upon? Of course we don't drink, so what will we do? Will there be anything for us to drink, or will we just stand there and die of thirst? Such silly questions. We never died of thirst. We usually found that there were some others joining us at the soft-drink table. We didn't feel anyone was snubbing us or looking down on us.

So what has this to do with the practice of hospitality in my own home? We found that we had to deal with some of the sticky, uncomfortable problems before they ever arose. For example, we are non-smokers (some might call us a bit militant about it). No one in either family ever smoked. It's fun to see the whole country coming around to our view. We cheer loudly at the new anti-smoking, clean-air laws going into effect in our state and around the country.

We truly do want our home to be a place where non-Christians, even smoking non-Christians, can come and be themselves. How can we do that when we hate the smell of cigarette smoke? An incident in our lives in Karachi illustrates this vividly. Through a long series of circumstances, I became friends with the sister of the then-president of Pakistan. She was suffering from irreversible cancer. She lay for months in a private room in the hospital and through a friend, I was introduced to her. She was a very high-class lady. But she sensed in me a true friend, one who truly loved her. I discovered that she loved American food, especially sweet things. I made her fresh peach pies, chocolate cakes, cookies, sweet rolls, candy—whatever I could dream up to share with her and bring her a bit of cheer. I talked with her, prayed with her, read Scripture with her. She shared her entire life with me.

As we moved slowly from cautious friendship to a deep loving and caring, she wanted me to meet her children, two sons and their wives. They, too, loved the goodies I brought. Mumti's cancer spread and she got worse and worse. We all knew there was no hope. One day her son called to tell me that they would be taking Mumti to London. A doctor there was experimenting with new anti-pain drugs and they had decided to use her in the tests. I was brokenhearted as I went to see her knowing full well I would never see her again. She was too sick by then to recognize me. I stood weeping behind an oleander bush as the ambulance came to take her to the airport. I knew that I had been faithful in sharing Christ and demonstrating His love to her. Even more clearly I realized that my responsibility had now shifted to her children who were left behind.

Shortly after her departure, I contacted one son and his wife. I already knew what my next step would have to be: invite them to my home to let them know how much we cared. I had no idea whether there would be an opportunity to share Christ verbally. I just knew what I had to do.

I also knew we faced what to us would be a big problem. All four of these young people were chain smokers. God had never given me the green light to preach to those kids about smoking. But He had given us as a family the incredible privilege of being friends to them. Our family talked about the problem. Do we meet them at the door and announce, "Sorry, folks, we don't smoke in this house"? We had to decide—before they came. Of course you know the result. We decided that it was more important for us to let down the bars, so to speak, and not make an issue out of the smoking than it was to stand our ground and risk offending these four precious young people. Looking back on it now, it really wasn't all that difficult to make the right decision. We had a delightful evening together. They loved our food. We had good, stimulating conversation. We had fun. We communicated Christ's love to them even though all four smoked one cigarette after another. I used cereal bowls for ash trays and all of them were full when they left. Every nook and cranny of the house smelled like stale cigarette smoke and it lasted a long time.

Was it worth it? By letting down the bars, did we have the joy of seeing them come to faith in Christ? To the first question, a resounding, "Yes, of course it was worth it!" To the next question, "No, they did not come to faith in Christ." We were not even free to share verbally a systematic outline of the plan of salvation with them. But we shared with them our home and ourselves. We showed them that we loved them, that we truly cared for them, and that whatever it was that we believed and lived by, it did give us the strength to reach out and truly care. Where are they now? We have no idea. We never heard from them again. But for one brief evening, in response to the clear prompting of the Holy Spirit, we had the unspeakable privilege of sharing in love our Christ-centered home with four hurting people. The political climate of the country changed dramatically and they were forced to flee. Was the evening a failure or a success? The answer to that question introduces another whole subject. There are other problems that must be faced.

When I have non-Christian people in my home, do I consider the time a failure if I have not verbally set down before them the claims of Christ? To put it more succinctly, have I failed if I have not emptied my "gospel gun" on them, realizing that I may never get another chance? In our success-oriented society, I fear that much of a worldly view has rubbed off on us. You see, we think we're responsible for the whole thing. Not that I minimize my responsibility to those who have not experienced Christ. That is our God-given responsibility, and it is an extremely important and serious one.

So many times we have had non-Christians on our own turf, our own home. What a perfect opportunity to manipulate every conversation. What an occasion for talking and not listening. But I can remember many times, especially the first times, when we spent an entire evening with non-Christians just getting to know one another. I remember one couple, teachers in our American school. They never would have agreed to go to church with us, but they did accept an invitation to dinner. Before we ever got to the point of inviting them, we got to know them through our children. It required sensitivity and the clear guidance of the Holy Spirit to recognize the moment when an invitation would be appropriate. As they arrived that first time, I quickly got the impression he was just waiting for us to unload the sermon on him. We could sense the wall he had built. He was tense and fidgety. She was nervous because he was nervous. I was a bit nervous because they were nervous. But as we sat at the table together, laughing, visiting and eating, his wall began to come down, bit by bit. He became less nervous, she became more relaxed, and so did we. We didn't tiptoe around in our conversation anymore. Immediately he began to talk about what he understood about Christianity. Then he talked about himself and we soon discovered why he was so cautious. Somewhere in the not-too-distant past a friend of his mother had determined to "get" this young man with her loaded gospel gun. She hadn't gotten him at all—she had turned him away.

As I think about those two now, I realize that even though that man had been turned off in the past, God had sown some seeds in his heart through her. You see, God can use our brashness, our insensitivity, our stupidity. He would rather we weren't that way, but He can go ahead and build on it anyway. By the same token, I am secure now in the knowledge that we also sowed some seeds, we also did some watering that night. Soon they left Karachi. I had to ask myself the question: "Can I really trust God to bring someone else into their lives to continue the watering process? Can I trust the Holy Spirit to use another Christian along the way to continue and perhaps finish this process begun here?" Of course I can. Every encounter with non-Christians in my home does not have to be a full-fledged church service where we begin and finish the job of preaching the Gospel. I have no doubt that such things do happen, but there must be sensitivity. This Spirit-filled sensitivity is not what we drum up on our own. It is the sensitivity that comes with the indwelling of God's Holy Spirit in our lives.

In emphasizing the need for Spirit-filled sensitivity, we do not want to go overboard the other way and overlook the importance of being prepared to explain the way of salvation when we *do* receive clear guidance from the Holy Spirit to share this with our non-Christian guests. Many Christians today have never led one other person to Christ and would not know how to go about it if suddenly faced with the opportunity. I cannot assume that you are fully prepared as a Christian to lead someone to Christ, even in the secure surroundings of your own home. Therefore, let me encourage you to know exactly how you would explain the gift of eternal life when you discern willingness on the part of your guest to know more about God.

Your ultimate goal in sharing your life and home with others is to draw them closer to God that they may come to know for themselves His love and saving grace. You may or may not be the one God chooses to lead them to a definite commitment to Christ in your home, but it is essential that you are able to share from the Bible a clear explanation of God's plan of salvation.

I have included at the end of this book a step-by-step explanation setting forth the basic truths concerning mankind's need of a Savior. If you are a beginner at sharing your faith and understanding of salvation, then learn these few points thoroughly. Familiarize yourself with a few related scriptures that you can refer to. (It would be best to take the time to memorize them.) Once you feel you have sufficiently mastered the basics, then further study how to share your faith. There are many good books available on the subject. Learn from others' experiences. And again I would encourage you to be creative and be yourself. Others will most likely listen to you talk about God when they can *see* His love working in your life.

Another matter that must be considered is praying before eating. We have never really felt this to be a problem, no matter who was at our table. After all, it's my home and even if there are people there from other religious persuasions, it is my right to begin a meal in the manner that suits my culture and religion. We have found that no one is bothered by saying grace before a meal. My husband always just says, "Let's ask the blessing," and people seem to know what to do. He makes it short and sweet, and I have noticed with interest that he adapts it to whoever is there. That is sensitivity.

How about having devotions, or at least prayer, before people leave? I think this is a very beautiful custom when Christians are involved. It can also be completely appropriate with some who are not Christians. Surely God's Holy Spirit can give each of us the sensitivity to know when it is right and proper. There are times when it could become the springboard for discussions concerning the things of Christ with non-Christians.

I am very thankful for recent books that give a lot of help in this area of informal, "friendship evangelism." Of special interest are Becky Pippert's *Out of the Saltshaker* and Joe Aldrich's *Lifestyle Evangelism*. I highly recommend both. I wish I had had them at hand when I first began keeping an open home. We are very conscious that we have experienced both success and failure in the practice of hallowed hospitality, especially when it comes to our dealings with non-Christians. We can only take the mistakes we have made and make them building blocks for a more effective use of our home. On the other hand, we don't labor under a burden of guilt concerning non-Christians we didn't verbally witness to in our home because we didn't feel free to share with them the whole gospel of God. We keep reminding ourselves that it is God's enterprise we are engaged in. There aren't easy formulas and procedures. The Christian life is a living out, a reaching out, a simple sharing through life and word. The Christian home is an effective means by which we can do this. Each must carry on this ministry within his own lifestyle, using his own abilities, and carefully tuning in to the Spirit of God.

The problem of liquor or wine in a Christian home is at the

forefront these days. It could be concluded that since the cocktail party mentioned at the beginning of the chapter afforded us, as non-drinkers, the option of having soft drinks or fruit juice, then I ought to afford the same choice to a drinker who comes into my home. Does it follow that since the hostess there did not try to force me to drink, then I should not try to force the drinker NOT to drink? I hope you can see the difference without my having to tell you. There is a difference. In the first place, I soon found out that none of our non-Christian friends died of thirst for liquor during the hours they spent in my home. At least they didn't let on if they did. During our time in Karachi, there was a controversy raging in the diplomatic and military community. There were some Christians, many who had never been away from home, to whom the ways of expatriots were completely new. Several Christians told us they had never had liquor in their homes, but now they felt it was required of them for the sake of their jobs and positions. In many cases, the results were disastrous. Some who had never touched liquor before went home as alcoholics. For some the sad effect came on their children. Many have not yet recovered.

You see, there is a difference. My home is my bastion, my castle, my turf. But more importantly, it is God's home and therefore I must be clear and firm about what will take place there. This principle enters into other realms of life as well, such as television, books, and magazines. We carefully thought through the whole problem of liquor, and on this basis we decided what was right for us. Actually, I don't think it is really as much of a problem as we sometimes think. A glass of iced tea or fruit juice is just as satisfying. Even those who normally drink have to admit they can enjoy an evening without alcohol.

So, in looking back we thank God for each individual who has been a part of our home and family for an evening, a meal, a weekend. I even can thank God for those who left behind a stench of cigarette smoke. We have been immeasurably blessed by sharing what God has given us, especially our lives in Christ. We have shared by our words when it could be appropriately done. We have shared with them what it means to be involved in Christian ministry. We have shared by giving them a glimpse into the life of a child of God. No, they didn't always understand what they saw and heard. And they didn't always respond. But we have tried to take each opportunity God has given us, and with the sensitivity of the Holy Spirit, we have carefully proceeded as far as that sensitivity would let us go.

Beyond that, we have tried to entrust to God and to other faithful Christians the next stage. As each has gone out from our house, leaving our immediate vicinity, we have entrusted them to God's care. He knows what has already been done in their hearts. He knows what they need next. And He even has the right person ready along the way to bring them on to the next section of their journey. I can trust Him. I can trust Him to lead me, to help me to speak, to help me to be quiet, and then to have another Christian ready along the way. Some plant. Some water. Some have the privilege of bringing in the harvest. But it is all God's work. Each stage is vital, but I don't have to do the whole thing every time. I just have to be faithful in the part of the farming process that God has given me. For me, the home is a fertile field.

Chapter Six

Who's in Control?

Several years ago, with the gentle prodding of my husband, I embarked on fulfilling a long-time dream. At the age of 50, I found myself accepted as a B.A. student in the field of Jewish Studies. You cannot imagine how world-shaking this was for me. It took every ounce of courage in me, plus a lot I didn't have, and much encouragement from the members of my family. Over and over again I experienced that strange mixture of excitement and paralyzing fear. I took one course after another, feeling more confident with each one. The arrival of the new catalog one summer brought the ultimate challenge: the study of the Hebrew language two afternoons a week. My husband found it hard to encourage me too much, but he was able to declare, "Well, may the Lord bless you real good." He had studied Hebrew in seminary and had not really enjoyed it.

I plunged in, terrified from the first. I would walk into class muttering to myself, "What on earth am I doing? I must have taken leave of my senses." Gradually I began to relax and enjoy every moment of classtime as well as the preparation time at home. My dream was being fulfilled: studying the Old Testament in the original language. Hand in hand with that unfolding dream was the awareness of something I had always known but needed to be constantly reminded of. My faith had never been seriously challenged. I had spent my entire life in a preacher's house, first as a child and then as a wife. I fit comfortably into the evangelical mold. If there was ever a "hothouse" Christian, I was one. I knew how badly I needed to be forced out of my tiny world, but I could always find the excuse that there wasn't opportunity. I knew the university setting would produce as much culture shock for me as our arrival as missionaries in Pakistan had 25 years earlier. I was absolutely right.

This Hebrew class was an unusual mix of Jews and Gentiles—liberal and orthodox—preachers, real scholars, and a few day-school students who were there simply because they needed four language credits. I knew I had the responsibility of being friendly and I felt quite comfortable with them all, except the liberals who called themselves Christians. I did not know how to relate to them.

By the end of the first year our class had dwindled from thirty to ten, granting us opportunity for great interaction with each other. When the second-year class was scheduled, the class was made up of the same ten as the year before. We greeted each other like long-lost relatives. Toward the end of the second year, we decided we should end the year with a party or a dinner. Our teacher, a lovely young Gentile woman, suggested that we also invite the department head, a practicing Jew. We knew he kept kosher, but we all agreed we should invite him anyway. To our delight, he accepted our invitation.

I invited them all, including their spouses, to come to our home for dinner. I cannot claim that my invitation was out of sheer joy of practicing hospitality. I think it was more that I am more comfortable in my own home and knew I would feel better if I had a bit more control. I had learned enough about all my classmates to know that none of us fit into any one mold. I knew the professor was more liberal than I. I knew the department head was a practicing Jew. Actually, I knew there were just two others who could have fit into my mold. We covered the full spectrum.

It was important that I know that, and here is the point of the story. My husband and I were aware of the potential for clash and confrontation in the makeup of that class. We knew we had the responsibility of seeing that nothing got out of hand during the three hours we were together, and we were determined that this special evening would not end in discord. To do this, we had to keep our "hearing aids" turned up in order to pick up every thread of conversation. As our friends arrived, we tuned up our antennas and prayed for the sensitivity we knew was necessary. As host and hostess, that was *our* responsibility.

Have you ever been involved in occasions with groups of people where without warnings things were out of control? Our evening could easily have turned out that way. In fact, it almost did, and it made me keenly aware of an aspect of hospitality that is so important.

The department head began to share stories of encounters he had had with various types of Christians and what he had learned about different groups. The more he talked the more ignorance he revealed, but we let it go. I began to feel uneasy and almost sensed what was coming. His next loud statement was: "I even heard of a Christian group that does not believe in using musical instruments!" Of course there are such groups—in fact, the pastor of one such church and his beautiful wife were sitting facing the speaker. The wife stood up and said so sweetly and confidently, "Yes, that's right. That's what we believe." I was proud and relieved. The department head was dumbfounded, and everyone else was uncomfortable. I really can't remember how we managed to get the whole conversation steered in another direction. We could have spent the evening clashing over the rights and wrongs of that particular belief but it would have been pointless and counter-productive. I didn't want her to feel offended; neither did I want to put our Jewish friend down. But it had to be brought to end or we could have had a very unprofitable evening on our hands.

My point is this. We must learn, as hosts and hostesses, to be aware of what is going on in our own homes as we practice Christian hospitality. I don't mean that we can never discuss things that might be controversial, nor do we always have to agree. But neither can we afford to let things get out of hand. I don't mind discussions on important subjects, but to spoil peace and tranquillity by endless arguing is not pleasant for anyone! I don't want that to happen in my home and I want to be on guard against it. It requires something of me. I want my guests to go away feeling they have been blessed, enriched, built up and stimulated. It is too easy to remember only the unpleasantness of such occasions, not the good things.

Another facet of control concerns the children—yours and your guest's. It is obvious that there are going to be occasions when the children are included in the invitation. At such times there is bound to be less formality than if they were not there. For some strange reason, children have a unique way of producing informality whether we like it or not. But children, uncontrolled and unchecked, can make an otherwise enjoyable evening a disaster. By the way, pets can, too, but that's a whole different subject. It is especially distasteful for people who have already reared their children or who don't have any to have an occasion spoiled by uncontrolled children.

I don't have a treasure chest full of tricks and techniques for keeping children under control. So much depends on the child, the parent, the house, and the occasion. But more than anything else, keeping children in line requires careful planning. It's too late to plan after the guests arrive. Make your plans ahead of time and be prepared for anything. If your house is small, I would guess that you will sometimes be tempted to lock all the kids in the closet and keep them there until it's time to go home. Don't! You must come up with some resourceful ideas to keep children out of trouble.

The ages of the children will determine whether it is best to set up a special table for them. Some children are too small to be separated from their parents. In that case, plan ahead. It's always good to have a high chair on hand, even if no one uses it when you are home alone. I personally think that every house should have a high chair, if not for your convenience, then for the convenience and comfort of guests who come with children. Telephone books piled on chairs are dangerous. High chairs can usually be found for a pittance at garage sales. Think of the relief of a mother who comes to find that she doesn't have to worry about holding her child on her lap while she eats. It is better for her, for the child, and for your carpet as well.

The same can be said for children who might need to go to sleep before the occasion is over. Maybe you can find out from your guests beforehand if any of their children will need a place to go to sleep. There are children, you know, who have a set bedtime and who go willingly no matter where they are. Mind you, I never had any who were that way, but some people do. Have the articles ready for making a place for visiting children to sleep. It doesn't have to be a special crib or child's bed, but whatever it is, have it planned ahead of time.

You really need to prepare your own children before the guests come concerning what you expect of them. Hopefully your philosophy of Christian hospitality is being transmitted to your children and they will be excited about being involved in this special ministry. But remember that even the best child is often adept at trying his parents' patience to its final degree when others are around. I am not saying that your well-laid plans for the children will always work, but try for your own sanity and that of your guests. Have toys ready for the kids to play with. Make it clear to your children that this is a sharing time. If you have areas of your house that are out-of-bounds for your kids, make that clear to the guests' children as well. Let them all— yours and theirs—know what their limits are. It is good for the adult guests also to know this. Unfortunately, this cannot be taught as a crash course one minute before the guests arrive. Hopefully, it will be the continuation of a process begun long before. Just remember, however, that children are not a lot different from adults—they need to be reminded over and over again of what is expected of them.

Our British friends have a custom that at first seemed strange to us. Often they will feed their kids around 6:30, then they read to them and put them to bed. After this they eat the main meal of the day, and it is usually at this time that guests are entertained. At first we thought it was awful that the children would be banished to bed while the adults enjoyed themselves. But, like most things, it has its good and bad side. While the child may be missing the time at the table with the adults, chances are that the parents will have been able to spend more quality time with them while the child ate his own supper. It is hard to give much attention to your children at the same time that you are entertaining guests, and children have a way of taking advantage of divided attention. It is probably better for the children not to have to suffer a nervous, fretting mother who all too often ends up losing her patience when the pressure builds up.

So, there are advantages and drawbacks. Probably there are times when the better part of wisdom calls for this time-tested British method. But in case you think it always works perfectly, let me remind you that even though the kids are tucked in bed, that isn't necessarily the last you are going to hear from them. I am reminded of a Dennis the Menace cartoon that always causes me to chuckle. The living room is full of chattering, happy adults. Down the stairway come Dennis and another child his age. Obviously they had been put to bed, not to be heard from again. As they come down the stairs in their drop-seat pajamas, Dennis says, "I like to drop the seat just as I walk into the room just for laughs." I know and you know it's much easier to talk about controlling children in the home than it is to actually control them. But we have to give it a try.

Children are wonderful ice-breakers. We found this so true during our ministry in Pakistan. But they are also skillful in breaking not only ice but a perfectly lovely occasion. My conclusion is this: Find some means of controlling your own children. It is much harder to control your guests' children, and that whole subject can open up a huge can of worms. You can always hope that when your guests control their children, it will rub off on yours. Or, vice versa. Perhaps when I have become a grandmother a few more times, I will be able to wax eloquent on that subject. But I'm not ready yet.

So control is important—over conversations (in a non-manipulative way) and over children. There is at least one more area of control—the television set. Just as it needs to be carefully controlled while you are alone with your family, it needs some checks on it when guests are there.

Recently a friend told me how they had gone to a friend's house for dinner with their children. The kids were shunted downstairs and it wasn't until they got home that she learned what her kids had been doing. They had been watching television—programs that were absolutely off-limits at home. Even the child was disturbed by what she had been viewing. Obviously the TV was not being controlled by anyone.

Of course we all realize that each occasion is different. And of course there are times when television watching is a part of the whole occasion. There is nothing wrong with inviting friends over to watch a football game or some other kind of program. But even then it must be under someone's control. As the host and hostess, it is our responsibility. It is a difficult one, but important.

Now perhaps in this discussion of sensitive control within the home you have concluded hospitality is too much trouble, if that's what's involved. Some might even consider the necessity of control a good excuse for never sharing their home with others, even though they know it is an important avenue of outreach. Perhaps there are those who decide that if it takes this much, it would be best to wait until the kids are grown.

I would simply say that it need not be such a big burden, and it should never be used as an excuse. This is an area where our Christian character is tested in a very practical way. If we can somehow remember that as Christians the Holy Spirit has been given to us to help us live out the life of Christ, it will help bring the area of control and hospitality into perspective. God is not the author of confusion. We should do all within our power to make our homes the reflection of Christ and His peace, orderliness, and serenity. But it is not easy. The peace and tranquillity of an evening of Christian fellowship can quickly be shattered by whining, uncontrolled children, by jarring of personalities, by endless arguing, or by uncontrolled television viewing.

Let's draw the lines a little tighter. I like to think of this as order and decency, both scriptural concepts. I am convinced that order begins long before the guests arrive. Planning and preparation will contribute to the orderliness of the whole occasion. Sometime sit in your living room or family room or wherever you are going to entertain guests. Survey the scene before you, injecting into the scene (in your mind's eye) what will happen when you add to your family, for instance, four more people—two adults and two children. Ask yourself these questions: What could I change to make entertaining my guests more orderly? Is there something I need to remove from the room to make more room? Is there something that needs to be removed for a child's sake (and of course for the mother's sake) to avoid the embarrassment of it getting broken? Could I change my furniture arrangement at all to make it more functional while guests are with us? How can I arrange and control the flow of traffic? What can I do to make my kitchen easier to clean after the meal?

Along with these practical things I find I need to ponder the interests and concerns of those who are coming. I wish I didn't have to confess this, but I do. I am not a good listener. I need to be and I know I need to work on it. It is just easier for me to talk than to listen. But I do need to know something about the people who are coming to eat at my table. Sometimes that isn't possible, but I should try. For instance, if one of my guests has strong, unbending opinions about ERA and I know that, it would be best not to mix that person with one who feels as strongly on the other side of the issue. It can be politics, sports loyalties, even theological positions. I just heard of a Christmas dinner that was completely spoiled by an ugly argument over divorce. One party took the hard and unbending view, one the more generous view, and caught inbetween was a poor young man who had just suffered through an agonizing divorce. Maybe it wouldn't have been possible to predict that bringing these people together was going to end in an argument, but someone needed to be controlling the situation. This is just a simple matter of careful planning and then of sanctified sensitivity.

So let's look over the entire subject and try to pull the strands together. Of course, the crucial element is sensitivity, produced by being controlled by the Holy Spirit. Husband and wife are controlled by the same Spirit; two roommates are controlled by the same Spirit. Further, they have a common goal, which is to make the occasion an object of true service to God. This makes the task so much easier.

The important thing is to remember that there is no set pattern, no "usual" when the Spirit of God is in control. Some people find it easy to make conversation; others find it exceedingly difficult, especially with people they don't know. Each is an individual, each has special gifts and abilities. Every individual, every married couple, every set of roommates, is unique and each must be sensitive to the control of God's Holy Spirit. The important thing is to find what you do well—whether you are married, single, male or female. As you make hospitality a habit and a way of life, you will quickly find what is best for you and will be amazed at how God will use your unique gift to produce enlightened conversation, uplifting discussion, and a sense of order and decency. The control of the Spirit of God is the most important thing.

So, just as each individual is different, so is each occasion. The more you practice hospitality in your home, the more natural the control is going to be. It is possible to develop a sixth sense in this regard. With much practice, a type of spiritual antenna activates when guests come into the home. You will naturally know how to lead and control when non-Christians come. You will know how to respond when you have a combination of Christians and non-Christians. You will be so in tune that this spiritual antenna will help you respond in just the right way in each situation. It is wonderful to be able to rely on God's Spirit to help you keep order.

One of the first songs I learned to play on the piano in the evangelistic style of another era was "Come Thou, Fount of Every Blessing." I love the verse that pleads, "Tune my heart to sing thy praise." Each day, in every activity, we need to go through this tuning process. Just like the concertmaster of a symphony orchestra, we must first get ourselves in tune and then be the instrument to keep people and occasions in tune.

So in the practice of Christian hospitality, constant tuning to the Spirit of God is required. Tuning comes through careful preparation, careful selection of the guests, and most of all, making each occasion a matter of earnest prayer. Then as we share our homes with others, Christians and non-Christians, the Spirit of God will help us to keep the occasion in tune as well.

Let's not minimize the need for stimulating, challenging conversation and discussion. We need to learn the art of open, peaceful and sensible discussion with one another. My concern is for the times when such occasions degenerate into verbal boxing matches. Some people have closed minds and some have open minds. Some have jangling personalities, some have peaceful personalities. Whatever the situation and whatever the mix of people, it requires some kind of control. Be sure that the whole occasion is under control.

Chapter Seven

Step-by-Step

Shortly after we were married, I discovered that my husband keeps a 3 x 5 card in his shirt pocket most of the time. It often goes through the wash. If it isn't in his shirt pocket or in pieces in the wash, it is on his desk at home. For a long time I resisted the temptation to peek at that card. One day I succumbed and quickly discovered that his memory was not, contrary to what I thought, any better than mine. He just transferred things to be remembered to the little card, while, alas, I tried to carry it all around in my head. As he gets the things done that he feels are important enough to go on the card, he scratches them off. He crosses off, adds new items, makes new cards, and in this way he keeps up very well. That is the key to his efficiency.

Are you asking what's on his list? Many, many things. In tiny, tiny scratchings he has carefully categorized items he wants to be sure to remember. Even such everyday things as putting the garbage cans out on Wednesday nights, cleaning and changing the furnace filters, changing the oil in the cars are there in one special place. But also there are more important things that could easily be forgotten in the rush of everyday life.

Are you asking what my husband's 3 x 5 card list has to do with hospitality? It has much to do with it. You see, on that little card are several lists of names. These lists are also categorized. Who are these people and why are their names there? In a sense, we could call these our entertainment register.

Have you ever said to your husband or wife, "We should have them over for supper sometime"? Or perhaps for dinner, or for tea, or after church, or out for pie with them. As often as not, we make the statement and then do nothing about it.

That's what my husband's categorized lists of people are for. One list has names of people we feel obligated to for some reason. I am sure you know what I mean by obligated. They had us over two months ago and we should try to reciprocate in some way. Actually, I know that love does not keep accounts, and I confess that I don't enjoy entertaining out of a sense of obligation as much as I do entertaining for the sheer joy of it. However, that obligation is what sometimes motivates me to practice Christian hospitality. Even though we know real love doesn't keep close track, yet we also know our love is far from perfect.

On another list there are names of people we want to reach out to. We really would like to have the opportunity of getting acquainted, and it seems that the home would be the best place. They might be new people in the church or new neighbors. For us it also means inviting the new students in Sam's classes at our college. This is especially pertinent for us at the beginning of the school year or the beginning of each new quarter. Another category would be those we would like to share our home with—perhaps someone we have just met, or would even like to meet. We do a lot of this kind of entertaining and find it very satisfying. Then of course there is the "old hat" bunch, close friends, whom we share with often. With them we can be at ease and share openly.

Another list contains those we want to invite with someone else because we feel we could be match-makers. Here I am not talking about romantic match-making (although that might be one consideration) but just the simple matter of bringing people together who would profit and be blessed by knowing one another. We especially love this kind of entertaining. From our own circle of friends we reach out and invite two people or two groups of people who have something in common and whose lives would be enhanced by knowing each other.

But let's get down to the practical application of hospitality, beginning with the list. Let's do a walk-through, run-through, practice run, or whatever you want to call it. Follow me through the logical and simple steps of an everyday matter like Sunday dinner. Incidentally, this is an ideal way to get started, and I hope that right now you will begin to make a list of people you would like to entertain at your table for Sunday dinners.

Where do we begin? Obviously we begin with a list. This list will help us move in the direction of really doing something about hospitality. We must begin by inviting someone. So, sit down right now and make a list of people you would like to entertain in your home in the near future. If you're newly married, a good place to start would be with your in-laws. If that strikes terror in your heart, then find another couple your own age, or also newly married. If you're single, begin by inviting another single to share your table. If you're a widower, find someone else who has experienced what you have been through. (I am tempted to say, "If you're a widower, invite a widow." That might not be a bad idea either.) Or, if you are single and you get tired of being with only single people all the time, find a couple to invite. There doesn't need to be anything exclusive about this inviting. The main thing is—invite someone. It moves us in the direction of Christian hospitality.

When you have made that decision, immediately telephone the people you want, warmly inviting them to join you for Sunday dinner. I realize this seems obvious and elementary. Indeed it is. But I know from experience that once I have taken that first step, I have provided myself with the extra motivation needed. I have started the ball rolling. There is no turning back, except for unusual circumstances. I am on my way.

In extending an invitation to anyone for any occasion, be as specific as you can about the time of day. Since various parts of the country use different terminology, be sure your invited guests understand that when you say "Sunday dinner," you mean "around noon" or "after Sunday morning church service." Being specific can save you and your guest embarrassment. I once invited friends from another country for Sunday dinner. We waited and waited. Finally, I called and found out that they had already eaten their noon meal and were planning to come for the evening meal, which at our house is nonexistent. My dinner was ready at 1:00, and they were planning to come at 5:00. That problem would have been avoided by my being very specific about the exact time. I learned a good lesson from that experience.

Having extended the invitation, next plan your meal. Personally, I find it easier to plan a whole meal than to plan for snacks after church or an afternoon tea. Since I have done it so much, it is routine. You will find yourself quickly settling into your own routine and will soon learn what is most convenient for you. In planning your meal, you will find a list is an excellent idea. Make a list of what you plan to have for dinner—a menu, if you please. Jot down all the items you need from the grocery store. It will make things easier for you.

What should be considered as you plan a meal for guests? Your budget. You alone know what you can afford. Sometimes you might find yourselves skimping a bit on your own eating to be able to splurge when you have guests. We do this a lot. No one else can decide for you how to manipulate and stretch your budget in order to be able to offer hospitality to others.

You might begin to plan your menu by getting out all your cookbooks. Some of us have just a few "old faithful" cookbooks we find never fail us. I have many cookbooks but I use only two on a regular basis. They are splattered and torn but I depend on them.

It just might happen that there are some who don't own a cookbook. For some of us that is hard to imagine, but I am sure it is true. If you are a single fellow, and you really would like to get started in the ministry of hospitality but don't have a cookbook, I have included some well-worn recipes in the back of this book. I have tried to pick recipes that are easy, economical, and don't require hours of preparation. You could start there. Or, I highly recommend such standard books as *The Joy of Cooking*, *Betty Crocker Cookbook*, or *Better Homes and Gardens Cooking for Two*. The bookstores are full—in fact, there are almost too many cookbooks. Make it easy on yourself. Start with the recipes you find in the back of this book.

Anyway, spend some time leisurely browsing through my recipes or someone else's cookbook. Look at the pictures, read the recipes. This is just to get ideas, to stir up your creative imagination. We usually begin by planning the meat dish or the casserole and building everything else around that. If you feel you can afford roast beef, roast pork, ham or turkey, just build the rest of your meal around that. Don't worry about books that say this vegetable doesn't go well with that particular meat. After all, that's your decision.

Be as creative as you know how to be. Don't think you have to use another cook as your guide. Be yourself and do what comes most easily for you. As you move along and practice this gentle art of Christian hospitality, you will find that you put your own stamp on all you do and that you have become an artist as surely as a painter or a musician.

Another consideration concerning your menu for Sunday dinner is how much time you have to prepare, to shop. If you work all day

Saturday, you need to think ahead about when you are going to prepare the meal. If you are a wife, you also need to consider how much help you can count on from your husband and your family. Perhaps you are the one who does most of the preparation, but it is always good to encourage your family, children as well as husband, to get involved in preparing the special meal. My husband does all the shopping after we have planned our menu, a project he thoroughly enjoys. I don't because I detest it. So we have an effective working relationship in this matter. The fact that he does the shopping leaves me more time for preparation. Of course, it might not be this way at your house. You may have to do it all. If you are single, you will have to do it all, which simply means that it can't all be left to the last minute.

If you live alone but still want to practice hospitality, how about finding another Christian friend who would like to share the joy of planning, preparing, and serving the meal to guests? This way you each can choose what seems the easiest item to make—it cuts down on the work for both of you. And of course, it is almost always more fun to share tasks and privileges with others.

If you are having a crowd in for a meal and one of the guests asks, "May I bring something?" don't be selfish. If you are sure the guest really wants to, make a suggestion as to what to bring so that the involvement can be in giving as well as receiving. Today when potlucks, covered dish dinners, dinner on the ground, or whatever you call them where you live, are so popular, this has made it quite acceptable and appropriate for almost any occasion.

If this is a new venture, I would suggest keeping it as simple as you can as you begin. For a roast beef dinner, there is nothing easier than roasting the potatoes and carrots with the meat so that they're all done at the same time. (When my daughter got married, she confessed to me that her biggest problem was getting everything done at the same time. She didn't know yet how to plan. But she is doing much better now.) Besides, I have never found anyone who doesn't love brown potatoes and carrots cooked in a roast. You don't even need to cook another vegetable with that meal—the carrots are enough. If you're from Missouri, like my husband, you probably feel strongly about having more than one vegetable. However, you don't have to make Missouri your example! A tossed salad or a simple gelatin salad, rolls, and fresh, crisp celery, with a simple dessert—is really all you need.

If you have decided to serve a casserole rather than meat as the main dish, you need to do even more careful planning. It's fun to experiment with casseroles from your favorite cookbook, but you do have to be careful because they involve more shopping than a simple meat meal. If your budget is slim, watch carefully as you study casserole recipes. Some of them contain so many items you don't usually keep in your pantry that they actually end up being more expensive. True, you have saved on the amount of money you have had to spend for the meat ingredient, but you quickly eat up your savings with cheese, soups, mixes, etc. So casseroles are not always economical.

Here's another suggestion. On occasion just spend some time in your kitchen going from cupboard to cupboard, from refrigerator to freezer to pantry. Carefully make note of what is already there. Let your imagination run wild and ask yourself the questions, "What kind of meal could I prepare for guests using ONLY what is now in my cupboards? What can I do for a meal without going to the grocery store?" You might be surprised. Things like macaroni, noodles, spaghetti, lasagna noodles—even small amounts—can become the basis for a respectable meal. How about the pound of hamburger stuck in the back of the freezer that could become the meat in a casserole? Maybe it is canned or frozen vegetables, cans of soup, or packages of different mixes you have been stocking up on as they have been on sale. Maybe you have left-overs from your refrigerator that could be mixed with other items to make a decent meal, even for company. Take inventory and think about what could be done with these items. So often we waste money, time, and energy because we don't bother to use what we have creatively.

Now let's move on to food preparation and the other necessary activities in getting ready for guests to come. We all want our homes to look neat and clean when guests arrive. I strongly recommend not leaving this chore to the last minute. (Obviously, I don't have small children around. I know cleaning is a thorny problem when you have a houseful of children who don't feel it is important to keep the house tidy.)

Even if you don't have children around, my advice is still: "Get ready ahead of time." In fact, I believe there is a psychological plus in being able to sit down in your living room and look around and know that your house is fit for anyone to enter. I am not talking about the kind of cleaning that requires scrubbing down the walls, washing all the woodwork, etc. The truth is, your guests are not coming to examine your housekeeping prowess. The things that are so obvious to you are not obvious to your guests. Do your very best to keep things in proper perspective. You may not believe this, but I have never yet (and we have entertained literally hundreds of people in our home) had anyone come into our house and begin to open cupboard doors and drawers to see that I am a behind-the-cupboard-door housekeeper. After all, doors are on cupboards for a purpose, aren't they? Your house can still look in tiptop shape even though you know what is behind those doors. Above all, don't talk yourself into using a messy or dishevelled house as an excuse for not entertaining. Just clean it up and dispose with that excuse. If that order is too big, you might even consider joining the organization known as "Messies Anonymous." I know some who have. However, it costs money and I feel sure that most people can solve the problem on their own. Just do what is necessary, and do the best you can. It's as simple as that!

Back to our Sunday dinner. I can best illustrate the preparation process by sharing the way we do it at our house. Maybe my process wouldn't fit at your house, but it will help to illustrate what I mean. You may even think I am in a rut. Maybe I am, but I have found what is easiest and most efficient for me in my own home. My routine has helped me eliminate the drudgery of preparation and entertaining. In fact, it's far from drudgery. It's fun! I want to help you experience the fun and joy of entertaining as well.

So here goes. I try to give my house a good cleaning sometime on Saturday. If I feel like it, or if I have activities on Saturday, I try to get started on Friday night. I almost always have my housecleaning done by Saturday afternoon. When it's all done, I sit down on the couch with my cup of coffee and just savor the scene—a house clean and orderly.

Remember what I said. I don't worry about what's behind the cupboard doors. What I can see I find pleasing. And remember what I said about the bathroom. Maybe my confession will encourage you. I hate cleaning the bathroom.

I make sure that my house stays clean for the rest of Saturday. My family knows they are under strict sentence if they don't keep it that way. It seems to me that's the least I can ask of them after I've worked so hard to get it looking nice. I am even more careful that everything is ship-shape before I go to bed. I simply can't bear to get up on Sunday morning to a messy living room, especially when I know I have guests coming after church.

Because I have done this type of entertaining so much and because of my own comfortable routine, my planning includes much more than what I am going to serve the guests for dinner. It also includes what tablecloth or place mats I am going to use, whether I will use good dishes or everyday dishes, goblets or tumblers, paper or cloth napkins. It will even include planning the centerpiece I will use. Since I enjoy this part of the preparation so much, there are many times when I can't even wait until Sunday morning. I often set my table before I go to bed on Saturday evening. I get a big kick out of getting up on Sunday morning and seeing my table all set and ready. It looks beautiful and it cuts down on what I have to do before and after church. If you have small children or pets this might not be practical at all. (We do have a cat. I think she knows better, but one Sunday morning I got up to find her sprawled out sound asleep in the middle of my carefully set table. You can be sure it didn't ever happen again.)

For my own peace of mind, I often like to have a lot of the food preparation done on Saturday evening as well. If I have planned gelatin salad, that gets done on Saturday. I remind myself to take the frozen bread dough (which I always use for rolls) out of the freezer to rise overnight. Then I can roll it out in the morning, stick the rolls in the fridge, pull them out when I get home from church, and I'm all set. Often I peel the potatoes, douse them in water, and stick them in the fridge on Saturday night. If I am running ahead of schedule, I even get the thickening for the gravy (we always have gravy—with everything) ready on Saturday night. It doesn't hurt it a bit. After all, it's only flour and water. I am careful to have the ice bucket and ice cube trays full. Sometimes I even have the pickles sliced and the butter and jelly in their fancy serving dishes before I go to bed.

Almost more important than anything else is the matter of dirty dishes. I don't have a dishwasher (nor have I ever desired one). This means that I can't stick the dirty cooking dishes in the sink! We have even gotten into the habit of never leaving washed and rinsed dishes in the drain. I don't want to face any extra work in the morning.

My first task on Sunday morning (remember the menu we started with) would be to brown the roast and get it ready for the oven. I don't have an oven with an exactly correct thermostat, but I know and understand it's little idiosyncrasies. I usually let it cook in the oven at a medium temperature for about two hours before I go to church. Then before leaving, I add the potatoes and carrots, put the lid on the pan, and turn it down to low. Sometimes I think I can smell the fragrance while I sit in church. Sometimes we all think we can smell the wonderful smell when we round the corner on our way home from church. I am sure it is our imaginations. But when we do get home, that wonderful roast beef dinner aroma permeates every nook and cranny of the house. The juice has turned a gorgeous brown, the meat is succulent and tender and just the right shade of brown, the carrots and potatoes are cooked to perfection. The juice is ready to be made into gravy and we are on the way to a glorious Sunday dinner.

The process I have outlined is an illustration of the need for organization ahead of time. The process would be much the same if I were fixing a casserole for Sunday dinner. Whether it be a favorite lasagna, chicken tetrazinni, or noodle bake, the process is the same. Casseroles usually take more work because of the cheese grating, onion chopping, opening cans of soups and packages of mixes, and cooking the macaroni or spaghetti ahead of time. You just have to plan for it ahead of time. The idea is to leave nothing until the last minute. By getting organized ahead of time, I can sit down with my guests and enjoy a relaxed, edifying meal with family and friends. I have by my careful planning eliminated the frenzy and fury of last-minute preparations. My meal is served hot and tasty, and it has been prepared and served with a minimum of fuss and bother, to say nothing of the fact that I have spared my family the unpleasant scene of a grumpy mother or wife.

Let me pass on another suggestion. Meats such as pork chops, swiss steak, barbecued ribs, or even fried chicken, take a different kind of planning. I don't often have them for Sunday dinner because they need to be prepared on the spot. I have never mastered the art of preparing fried chicken in the oven, although I know many who have. For Sunday dinner, I make it my first priority to prepare the food ahead of time and have it cooking while we are away from the house for three hours. I also like to be able to concentrate on the Sunday school lesson and church service without the distractions of wondering if the chicken is going to be too crisp or the chops too done. Those dishes can be prepared at other times when I have two hours at home before the guests come. That, of course, is just my opinion, born out of experience.

We have discussed the preparation and partaking of a meal. Now we face the real hang-up—the excuse we use for not doing what we know we should do—cleaning up after the meal. It isn't enough to invite the guests, get things organized, go through the whole process of preparation, serve the meal, accept the praise and the thanks of your guests, and then get up from the table. You know as well as I do that tables don't clear themselves, and kitchens don't clean themselves. Perhaps the hardest part for many people is what comes after it all. After the euphoria of having really succeeded in putting on a tasty meal in an appropriate manner, after the "high" of having people rant and rave about your wonderful food, there is always the dreaded chore of cleaning up. You might even have made the decision not to entertain in your home because you don't like the hassle of cleaning up after it is all over.

If your guests are acquaintances or good friends, there is almost always a genuine offer of help from someone. If you have children in the home who are used to helping, you probably have the solution to your problem. If you want them to help, it is probably best to do it after the guests have left. However you choose to handle the situation, just remember, cleanup must be done. Come to grips with that before you ever begin. If it has become the black cloud lurking over you on every occasion of entertainment, ask God to help you.

However you do it, you know what suits you best. If you are entertaining several guests or another single person, you may prefer leaving the table and continuing your fellowship in the living room. We must remember, though, that it is quite possible to have meaningful and stimulating conversation with hands in the dishwater— sometimes it is even better. If you are entertaining a couple, most kitchens are large enough for four people, and the job goes more quickly. I have known occasions where even two husbands would offer to do the mop-up so the women could relax. But it just might be that you would really prefer to do the cleanup alone—in your own way, at your own pace. Sometimes I prefer doing it alone; other times, I like help, and I know I can always get it.

At any rate, I am the one who has to decide whether or not to accept the offer. If you do choose to wait, I strongly suggest rinsing the dishes off and putting the silverware into a pan of hot soapy water. It makes the final act of dishwashing much easier.

If you choose to clean up alone, make the time of fellowship special between you and the Lord. For those of you who are fortunate enough to have a dishwasher, it won't be such a big problem. If, like me, you don't have one, you will have to deal with it in some other way. At least a window near the sink can help to make the time go faster. I have, of all things, a mirror above my sink. I use it to remind me to meditate and commune with the Lord during the dishwashing chores. I find myself treasuring those moments alone, hands in the warm water, head bowed—just my Lord and I in close fellowship.

I love those moments when everything is neat and orderly again, the kitchen ship-shape, my hands tingling from the warm, soapy dishwater, my heart full of love and praise to God for the joy of fellowship and the privilege of sharing my home, and deep satisfaction that I have accomplished what I set out to do. I have been blessed by the company of others, and I have had the unique opportunity of being involved in the practice of Christian hospitality. Those moments have earned me my Sunday afternoon nap.

So begin, first by making a list, then by selecting someone from that list and making the phone call. Next, pull out the cookbooks, get your creative energy in gear, do the necessary planning and preparation. Plan ahead, get organized, and begin to move. Ask God to make your home a peaceful haven, a place of serenity and quietness, a means by which He can show His love to others.

No, it isn't going to be easy the first time. As you move ahead, however, you will find yourself developing a unique style—your own system, your own organization, your own special touch. From these very important "your owns" will come a harvest of blessing and satisfaction, to say nothing of a means of ministry.

So get started—and get started now!

Chapter Eight

Focused Ministry

A recent issue of one of our favorite Christian periodicals, *His Magazine*, carried an editorial that elicited from me a hearty "Amen."[1] I liked it so much I wrote the editor a letter. This editorial helped galvanize my thinking about the qualities required in a true servant of God. The editor wrote about standing in the Press Box at the Urbana Missionary Convention, listening to the Bible teacher make a very radical statement: "If God called you to be a servant of the Gospel and instead you became President of the United States, that would be a dreadful comedown." The editor went on to tell of his feeling of resentment at the fact that two of his best friends had said they would be willing to go any place on this earth if God called them—even the faraway, undesirable places where their unusual talents would be wasted. As he analyzed the reasons for his resentment, he came to the conclusion that it sprang from the feeling that his two friends were really too good for that. As I read his editorial, I had to chuckle, because as I looked deep inside myself, I would have concluded the opposite—they were just too good to stay at home.

In the remainder of the article he explained the qualities that in his mind made his friends too good to go overseas. One of the qualities he saw in both his friends was a sincere liking for people. He called one of his friends a "pathological extrovert by nature." Evidently his friend had the ability to channel his sincere liking for people into an intentional effort to reach out to his neighborhood and his apartment

---

[1]David Neff, "Bad Thoughts," *His Magazine* (April 1985), p. 32.

building. He had committed himself to getting to know the very ones missions-minded people may overlook.

He cited examples of this quality in his friend. Christmas becomes an opportunity to invite neighbors over for food and to sing carols. A passing complaint about a toothache from a girl across the hall becomes an opportunity to ask if she would like him to pray for her.

This editor ended his article by saying that the very things that made his friends the best here at home are the same things that God can use to make them great for the Gospel in another culture. And I would add that the same qualities that equip an individual to reach out in another culture are the ones that make a person useable in this culture.

The crux of the matter is not whether a person stays at home to minister or goes overseas, but that each of us cultivate in our daily lives a sincere liking for people and a commitment to touch them wherever we are. Surely there is no one place to practice and cultivate this trait. It is one thing to have a sincere liking for people. It is quite another to find the ways and means and the motivation to reach out to them in love and care. Pathological extroverts we need not be. Liking and loving people we must. Each of us expresses that love and concern in different ways. Some people are by nature quiet and unassuming. Others are by nature gregarious and outgoing. God can use one as well as the other, and again, the combination of our homes and our lives can make a vital difference in this world.

May I be so bold here to add a special word to American men— especially men in the evangelical wing of the church. For some strange reason, the idea is prevalent that some types of ministry are reserved for women and some for men. When we talk about the gift and ministry of helping others, it is usually women who are addressed. When it comes to the gift and ministry of encouragment, we usually think of women, working quietly behind the scenes, in their proper place.

While it is not my purpose here to engage in a discussion of the whole matter of women in ministry—what they can do and what they cannot do in the evangelical church—I would like us to look at the reverse side of the coin—the things that men ought to be engaged in. I have tried to show that hospitality can and should be looked upon as a vital means of ministry. To the men I would say this: don't assume that it is just for women. Don't come to the erroneous conclusion that the gift of hospitality is given only to women. For husbands and wives, I believe strongly that it is one of the ministries that should be shared. There really is nothing wrong with breaking rules that are purely cultural, as long as in so doing we are more clearly demonstrating God's love.

There is nothing our Lord enjoyed more or did more beautifully than shocking people by His very special treatment of women and children. He treated them as equals in God's kingdom. He really did. If Jesus wasn't afraid to break the traditions of the culture around Him, neither should we be afraid to go against the grain of our cultural mores. This might even require men getting deeply involved in showing hospitality in the home, and all that entails. It matters not whether this hospitality is practiced in the home, in the church, in ministry to the poor and downtrodden, to senior citizens, to internationals—it is for both men and women.

Here is a word of warning, however. We need to guard against a love that in effect declares, "I want to serve you and love you because you need me—you need the Gospel I have, the encouragement I can give—you need my help." Our love must be unconditional, whether people reject our Gospel, our counsel, or turn their backs on the message.

Just as we each must decide what will be the particular style of our ministry through the home, so we must also decide who will be the primary focus of our attempts at Christian hospitality. There are clothes that are just not "me," there are lifestyles that are not "me," and there are modes of entertaining that don't fit me at all. By the same token, we need not all zero in on the same categories of people when we practice hospitality.

In addition to the entertaining we do just because we love to be with our friends, there are some special categories we can become involved in. Some people have unusual and effective ministries through their homes with senior citizens, others with internationals, others with college students, some with children. And then there are those who have been especially gifted to use their homes in evangelistic hospitality. It doesn't necessarily mean they do nothing else. It just means that this seems to be a unique ministry they are engaged in.

Along with different groups of people, there are different underlying purposes for the practice of hospitality. The most common is undoubtedly the occasions when we get together for pure fellowship. The apostolic church was characterized by fellowship, or *koinonia.* They needed it in a world hostile to them. We also need it. We neglect Christian fellowship to our great peril. Surely included in the fellowship aspect of hospitality is the need for encouragement— you encourage me as you come to my home, and hopefully I am able to encourage you. We are building each other up. Unfortunately, this is not automatic. Sad to say, what we call "fellowship" does not always include encouragement. But it's what we should aim at.

Further, there is also the need for evangelism, which in many cases can be done best in our homes. Of course we ought to be "doing evangelism" wherever we are—at work, at school, out traveling. But there is a different and more effective focus that comes as we open our homes. I thank God for those in the family of God who have special gifts in this regard.

Let's look at some special categories of people to whom we can have distinctive ministries.

1. *Senior citizens.* Sociologists say that 10% of all senior citizens in America are now living in nursing homes. Add to that number the older people who still live in their own homes or apartments, yet who are all alone and need love and care from someone special. Many of these people, who have lived full and productive lives, feel abandoned by the rest of society. This is especially true for those removed from family and loved ones. Why not check with the nursing home or the senior citizen high-rise nearest you and see if you can make a regular ministry of bringing a few of these people to your home once a week or once a month? My sister is involved in this in the small town where she lives. She often invites them for Sunday dinner, and their joy at being in a home with a family makes all the effort worthwhile. This ministry can be carried even further by getting involved in arranging picnics and outings for these people, or taking them on shopping trips. Each of these activities surely comes under the category of "hospitality," especially since part of the definition is "friendly and solicitous entertainment of guests."

2. *College students.* At this particular stage of our lives, my husband and I find having our college students over the most practical aspect of showing hospitality. Of course that isn't all we do, but it is easiest for us. Being part of a college family of nearly a thousand makes it quite simple. It could become a full-time job. Even though our two daughters are no longer college students, we still do more of this type of entertaining than anything else. Our daughters used to bring their college friends home in droves. Now we try to invite those who are in Sam's classes.

Does it take a special type of person to have college students around? Yes and no. Yes, because if there is one thing that college students want from those who are older, it is acceptance. You don't have to agree with everything they say and do. They do want you to listen to their ideas and relate to them as equals. Listening is crucial. They want to know that you don't have all the answers on every subject. They want you to be as teachable as you expect them to be. This is the attitude that keeps the door of interaction and communication open with students. And frankly, we need them as much as they need us. They help us keep things in perspective, as well as young in spirit.

A pastor once wrote: "Few things are more pitiable than a college sophomore stuck several hundred miles from the tender loving care of home. At least, that was true of me. But a simple act of brave hospitality showed me Christian love as I have wished to see it ever since." He goes on to tell how during that college year he came down with mononucleosis. He was very sick and didn't know what to do. A quiet, unobtrusive family from the church where he worshiped asked him to come to their house to recuperate. With plenty of tender loving care he regained his health, and after a week he was able to wobble around on his own. God might not ask you to be engaged in such heroic hospitality as that, but you might find a very satisfying and rewarding ministry with college students, well ones as well as sick ones. This pastor remembers that the hospitality offered to him flavored his whole spiritual formation during those years. Through their gourmet meals, popcorn snacks and barbecues, they were in effect saying, "We love you and want to be with you." He felt honored—they were blessed. They helped him belong. He became family.

There are no doubt hundreds of students who would love an opportunity to get out of the chaotic dormitory atmosphere to experience the sights, smells, sounds, and feel of a truly Christian home. Actually, it is an easy type of entertaining to get involved in because students don't care if you set an elegant table. They don't care about gourmet food. More than anything else they want to be made to feel at home. They want a laid-back, unstructured, informal atmosphere. They want to be with families. They don't shock easily when your beautiful salad remains in the refrigerator because you forgot to serve it. They don't need to be entertained. They like to watch a football game, read the newspaper, or best of all, stretch out on the floor and fall fast asleep.

Our daughter once brought a young man home for Sunday dinner. In a long discussion that took place around the table and after dinner, this bright young student was quite impressed that Sam had not put him down when he had come up with the other side of an argument. "He didn't put me down—he listened to my position." We make Sunday noon and afternoon a time for students to be completely at ease with us, even though they are often students from my husband's classes. It is good for them to see him in his home and interact with him in a different way. The reverse is also true.

So maybe it doesn't take a special personality at all. But it does require an abundance of acceptance, caring, listening, sensitivity and deep respect for who students are. Most important to students is that for those few hours, they feel like they're at home.

3. *Internationals.* Today we live in a world on the move. A continual flow of people—individuals and groups—wanders around the face of the earth. Modern-day transportation makes it possible for us to have breakfast on one side of the globe and dinner on the other. All of this has affected the way we live and the way we look at the rest of the world. It has put us in touch with a vast mission field right here at our own doorstep. We no longer have to go to them—they have come to us. Consequently, each of us has to decide what is our Christian responsibility to these strangers in our midst. Nothing beats the truly Christian home in our ability to touch and affect these people. Along with our sending, our praying, our giving for missions, we can be involved right here at home.

In the U.S. today there are thousands of foreign citizens temporarily here on educational assignments. Add to the students the people who are here in business or for political purposes and those who are refugees, and practically every nation and culture in the world is represented. Moreover, we can add the visitors to our country who come each year just to travel for entertainment or education.

What is our responsibility to them? Do we bring the scriptural command to "entertain strangers" to bear on our interaction with these people? Most certainly. We can and should have a profound influence. We can have a negative influence. But hopefully we will most often have a positive influence. Many of these strangers will return to their homelands and have a significant part in shaping the futures of their respective countries. This clearly illustrates the ripple effect of the faithful witness of individuals in God's plan of evangelism.

How do we affect them negatively? If they are Christians, they may not be impressed by the materialistic edge so visible in American Christianity. They may be affected adversely by a general lack of friendliness and deep caring and helpfulness on the part of the host country. On the other hand, the friendliness, genuine care and concern and love shown to a foreigner can make the difference between the person returning home with a better view of Christianity rather than the opposite. He could return to his own country more opposed to Christianity than before, or he may return with a new sympathy and understanding, or best of all, with a personal relationship with Jesus Christ. There is nothing like a warm and loving Christian home to bring him to this point.

Again does it take a special personality or a special gift to reach out in hospitality to these representatives of other cultures in our midst? Again the question requires a yes and no answer. There are guidelines and cautions that need to be dealt with.

Remember, many foreigners have never in their entire lives had personal contact with a true Christian. That puts a heavy responsibility on us. Sometimes these guests have been warned that there will be some in America who will try to convert them from their own religion (if, indeed, they have any real religion). They have been warned. So we need to consider the attitudes common among internationals as we seek to reach out in love, understanding and friendship. Once we are aware of these things, we can determine the positive points and attitudes to be demonstrated in our contacts.

Careful research of the attitudes common among internationals reveals some interesting things. There is one thing common to all internationals, no matter what culture they come from. It is their desire, above everything else, to have in America at least one genuine friend. By "friend" they don't mean a casual acquaintance with the person who sits next to them in class at the university, or the person who waits on them in the supermarket, or the landlord they rent from. By "friend" they mean someone willing to be close enough to them that they feel free to share their deepest longings, their problems, their achievements, their perplexing questions. Casual friendships are not hard for them to find—true friends are. What a glorious opportunity for Christian students, Christian business people, and just ordinary Christian families to tap this desire.

So, who should engage in this type of friendship hospitality? Obviously, it's easiest for members of the college or university community to get involved. But it is not limited.

Imagine for a moment that you live in an apartment building. You discover that the newest renters in your building are from India. You know they are different. Exotic and sometimes offensive smells waft down the halls from their apartment. You know they are eating foods different from yours. My husband's sister and her husband have had just this experience within the past year. A young couple from India, Sikhs by religion, moved into the apartment upstairs. The husband has a good job in the town. The young wife is left home alone. Since they came to the U.S., a baby was born. In Indian culture, the birth of a baby is a time when the whole family is around the home. Mary Kay determined that she was going to do all she could to make these people at home, especially at the time of the birth of the baby. As time went on, these two couples have become not just casual friends. A deep relationship has evolved. Mary Kay makes some of her famous soup and takes it upstairs. She has helped with the care of the baby, especially during those first weeks. They help them with their shopping. They have included them in Christmas celebrations. Now others in the apartment building have gotten involved and the circle of friendship has widened to include other Indians.

Who has profited by all of this? Surely the Indian family has been helped immeasurably by a close and caring relationship with an American Christian family. Families in India have been involved through correspondence, gifts, pictures, etc. Other Christians have gotten in on the act. Who knows where this will end? So, a family need not have contact with a university or college in order to minister to foreigners. Further, it isn't even a prerequisite that you have a college education at all. Foreigners in our country are anxious to meet people from all walks of life and all economic levels. Where better to carry on this ministry than from your home? Age is no barrier. They highly respect older people in other cultures. They love children. They love young people. They just want to get to know Americans.

Fortunately, if you are new to this type of entertaining, there are helps available both from organizations that specialize in ministries to internationals and from books.

There is always the potential for embarrassing mistakes in such a ministry. The embarrassment can be from both sides. Perhaps a few general tips will help you avoid these mistakes.

1. Make your invitation clear and definite. Terms like "lunch,"

"supper," or "dinner" need to be accompanied by a time, since those terms mean different things in different cultures. Also, you will usually need to pick foreign students up because they usually don't have cars.

2. In the beginning, it is perhaps best to invite two for the visit rather than just one. They are more at ease with one another, and will be more at ease with you. It isn't always possible to have two from the same country, but it is less stressful if you invite two who already know each other. Here it is also good to realize that sometimes it can even be a problem if your only criterion for inviting two at a time is that they share the same religion. Islam, for instance, does not produce genuine unity, even in this country. I heard of a Christian family who sought hard and long to find two Muslim students to invite at the same time. One was from Egypt, a real Muslim fundamentalist, the other, from Iran, a thorough-going Muslim liberal. The two of them spent the evening arguing about their opposing ideologies, and the hosts were caught in between, understanding very little of what was going on.

3. Try to find out if there are dietary restrictions that you should know about. For instance, Muslims and Jews do not eat pork (the more liberal ones might have succumbed but it is best to play it safe), and good Hindus do not eat beef. Many Hindus are strict vegetarians and it is much better if you know ahead of time that they are not going to eat your expensive, carefully prepared roast beef. Usually lamb, chicken and scale fish are quite safe for most foreigners. Since rice is the staple food for most of the rest of the world, that is also a pretty safe bet. They usually are not used to the kinds of sweets we serve for desserts, although ice cream is quite popular the world over. They seem to prefer fresh fruit after the meal.

4. If they arrive wearing native dress, don't be shocked. Ask them what it is called, the significance of each piece, and let them know that you appreciate their helping you to understand their culture. A few years ago we befriended a young Muslim girl from Egypt who was studying at the university. It was winter, and when we picked her up she had her long hair all piled up into a wool cap, which I assumed she would discard when she got to our house. She explained to me that she always kept her head covered. She had on a long wool skirt and a high-necked, long-sleeved sweater. She was completely covered. As we got acquainted with her we found she was a devout Muslim. When I asked her what she had found to be most

offensive in her dormitory on the university campus, she told me without hesitation, "It's the so-called Muslim girls from Iran who don't cover their heads, who don't cover their legs, who smoke and drink, and act like American girls." Well, that was a surprise.

5. Entertain simply and be yourself. There is no need to entertain elaborately. Your way of entertaining will be so different from what they are used to anyway that it really won't matter. Remember that they may come from cultures where everyone eats out of one bowl in the middle of the table or from cultures where the host and hostess never sit at the table with the guests. Anything we do is going to be strange to them, so there is no need to waste time and effort and money making it elaborate. Most of all, they want to be relaxed and made to feel at home and a part of the family. They like to be able to fit into a routine and not made too special.

6. Be sure to invite them back. It isn't enough to say, "Just call us when you have free time and we will come and get you." Chances are they won't and you will have lost the opportunity. The responsibility is on you to keep up the contact. Remember they are the guests. Find out when they are leaving the country and do something special to say good-bye. Of course it goes without saying that we should do all within our power to keep up the contact even after the person has left America. Letter-writing will be the God-given avenue of keeping up the contact.

7. Develop spiritual sensitivity in the area of witness and evangelism. We need to be careful about forcing religious discussions on them. On the other hand, we need to be alert to any opportunity God may give us to respond to them in a spiritual way. In most Eastern cultures people are used to having things done for them in order to get them "under obligation." There is sometimes a hidden agenda. They also have these ideas about us. They may be asking themselves, "What is his motive for asking me into his home?" They may even suspect that you would like to convert them. Because of this there is a need to build confidence and rapport, and in turn to be sensitive, tactful, and extremely patient. Religious discussions must be carried out with extreme wisdom, tack, and diplomacy. Another important point to remember is that if we get into discussions of spiritual matters, we do not reject them if they refuse to accept our message. Somehow we must make them know beyond the shadow of a doubt that we want them as our friends and that this friendship will not end because they refuse to accept our message. This will take the tension

out of our encounters and allow the Spirit of God to do His work in His way. And remember, we have not failed if we do not have the joy of leading them to Christ. God really can be trusted with the results of our attempts at evangelism.

8. Don't insist that they attend church with you. If they express an interest, by all means make them welcome. Hopefully you will have a church family who will be sensitive to their needs and who will at least be friendly—but not too friendly. Guard against embarrassing them in any way. Let them be just observers.

9. In conclusion, deep relationships with internationals, whether through home, school, or business, but especially through the home, usually require a continuing commitment. We have friends who have made this the focus of their long-term commitment to Christian hospitality. God is touching the lives of internationals through this family. Their involvement has even gone to the extent of inviting a student from mainland China to live with them. He is a part of their family. He is having the experience of observing over a long period of time through daily living what a Christian lifestyle really is. Only God knows what the end result will be. He can be trusted with the results.

Don't forget one final type of hospitality I mentioned earlier. Seek to bring people together—for fellowship, for information, for encouragement, for life direction. We might call it "matchmaking"—the joy of bringing people together who need to know each other. Maybe they have the same interests, maybe they are headed toward the same school, maybe toward the same type of ministry. Have you ever heard yourself or someone else saying, "Oh, you should meet my friend. You and he would have so much in common"?

We recently made a match. A veteran missionary couple to Japan had been on furlough for a year, living near us and worshiping at our church. They were ready to leave to return to their work in Japan. We wanted to have them for a last meal with us before they left. We also have in our church a young couple, both full-time students, who hope eventually to go to Japan as missionaries. We decided it would be good to have both couples at the same time. They needed to get to know each other. The young couple could ask whatever questions they wanted to in the informal atmosphere of our home. The veterans were able to pass on good advice about training, commitment, and what the couple eventually would be involved in. We didn't keep our agenda hidden at the time we invited them. We told both couples that we thought they needed to get acquainted. It was a delightful time.

Right now we have the names of two young couples on the list of people we want to invite. They are both headed for Pakistan as missionaries. We not only want to get to know them so we can pray more intelligently for them, but as veteran missionaries to Pakistan, we will be able to help them immensely as they prepare for missionary service. It's fun to share our home in this way, and even more fun to share our friends.

Along with what we do in and through our homes for our friends and acquaintances, our neighbors and our co-workers, we all need to be involved in a special ministry to groups such as senior citizens, students, or internationals. No, we can't do everything. But we can all do something.

You will notice, I am sure, that I have left out one category of people who greatly need to be recipients of gracious Christian hospitality: missionaries and Christian workers of all kinds. I have done that in order to devote an entire chapter to this ministry.

Chapter Nine

Room for the Prophet

I can pinpoint exactly the moment when I fully realized that I was no longer a missionary, in the usual sense of the word. It was exactly one year after we had come home to take up new responsibilities, this time in the teaching profession. We knew we had done the right thing, most of the time. We were still very much involved in missions in our new position. In fact, we were on a leave-of-absence for a year to have time to adjust, to think, and to pray about the change from "there" to "here," especially with respect to its permanence. In time our leave-of-absence changed to a resignation from the mission. But at the national meetings of our denomination held that year in our city, we had the privilege of attending sessions, meeting new missionary appointees, and renewing acquaintances with friends from all over the world. We felt that at long last we were really back in circulation.

Our mission board sponsored a women's luncheon for furloughing missionaries, new missionary appointees, retiring missionaries, and in fact, all the women of our constituency. During the course of the luncheon, all the missionaries were asked to stand. At that moment it dawned on me that we were no longer part of "the ranks." Although still very much involved in missions, in a different way, we could no longer be counted a part of the missionary family of our denomination. The effect of that discovery was as traumatic as anything I have ever gone through. To me I had in one fell swoop moved from being somebody to nobody. I was a has-been. Now, you don't have to tell me that attitude reflected some wrong thinking about involvement in God's service, but that's just how wrong I was. The point is that I felt unsure and insecure about where I now fit in.

I've shared that experience with others who have gone through the same thing. To my relief, I discovered that others experienced the same reaction. If you would ask "why," I would simply have to say that the missionary community is a close, and I am afraid, sometimes closed community. There is a camaraderie that exists among missionaries and among their children that can't be duplicated. I often invite missionary kids from our college to share a meal with us. Sometimes I mix them with non-MK's. In that situation, everyone behaves alike. But when we have a tableful of MK's we observe a culture that is unique: they are an interesting and often complex subculture. The MK's are at ease with one another, even though they might be from different cultures. They interact differently with each other than with those who don't share their backgrounds.

When we speak of missionaries, whether on the field or on furlough or even retired, and also when we talk about that special group of young people known as MK's, we must be careful about stereotypes and generalizations. I find myself seething when I hear missionaries or MK's maligned as a group. Much harm has been done to these special ministers of Jesus Christ by making broad generalizations about them. It is wrong to generalize and make missionaries or MK's too saintly. But the opposite is also wrong. Actually, we cannot make any statement that will be true of each missionary. We dare not make a categorical statement that missionary kids are "this" or "that." Missionaries and MK's are, first of all, unique human beings, just like all of us. Spending long periods in cultures different from ours has helped shape and mold them, just as our culture helps form those of us who live here. We have no problem agreeing that in our churches there are groups of people who have different needs. Missionaries as a group also have unique needs. I can think of churches that carefully discern and address the needs of children, teens, singles, single parents, internationals, and senior citizens. It also follows that there should be those within the Christian community who have a special ministry to furloughing and retired missionaries, appointees, and most surely to missionary kids.

Let's look at some of the distinct needs of this group and see again how the Christian home can be used of God to minister to them in a special way. Perhaps you have never thought that you might have a special ministry to missionaries. You may assume they don't need your help. You do not need to fuss over them, but you do need to see their special needs and problems and then decide if indeed God has this ministry for you.

Any discussion of missionaries and their needs and problems must begin by addressing the subject of culture shock. We are all creatures of our own culture, whatever it may be, whether we like it or not. As we grow up we are unconsciously nailing together a raft of familiarity that helps us to ride the waves of our own society. We each develop our own strategy for coping—one that works well for our own culture. We plant our feet firmly on what we consider normal and there we stand. "Culture shock," then, sums up all the complicated emotions we feel when the planks of our raft begin to separate.[1]

Now, consider the missionary. He has grown up in a Western culture, knowing how to cope. He suddenly, often overnight, is whisked away to a culture where nothing is the same. He experiences severe culture shock. The raft of familiar actions and responses he has known for his whole life splinters and floats away. As he sees his raft begin to break up, he looks longingly for each familiar splinter of wood. Someone has well said that culture shock can make the most committed missionary feel like quitting, but it can also be a positive learning experience.

While this dreaded experience of culture shock takes place as the missionary leaves home and finds himself in a strange culture, the same thing also occurs when he comes home. By the end of a four-year term, he has gone through the romance and honeymoon of being a missionary, reacted to it, recognized it, and learned to cope with it. In essence, by the time of his first furlough he has probably learned to live, more or less, with the culture in which he finds himself.

So what happens when he comes on his first furlough? You may find this hard to believe, but we have found that with missionaries facing their first furlough are two conflicting emotions. One is excitement and anticipation at the thought of going home, eating American food, seeing loved ones, being away from the strange languages, sights, sounds, and smells, getting good medical treatment, and worshiping in familiar services and surroundings. It is almost overwhelming the first time. I can vividly remember our first real church service

---

[1]Stephen Hoke, "Culture Shock," *World Christian* magazine (Nov/Dec 1984), pp. 26-28.

after we arrived on our first furlough. I couldn't sing, I couldn't pray. I just wept. It was totally different from what we were used to in our little desert home. Missionaries find themselves counting first the months, then the weeks, then the days, and then the hours to the time they return home. Half the fun of furlough, just like half the fun of vacation trips, is the planning.

But running parallel to the excitement and anticipation are fear, bewilderment, and sometimes downright dread. That dread can become paralysis by the time the departure date arrives. What is the basis of this fear and dread? It is usually that somehow you will no longer fit into American society, that you will look and behave like a country bumpkin or a dowdy frump, that you won't have an intelligible and successful report to your churches and supporters, and most of all that you won't be accepted because you have been away too long. In short, it is culture shock in reverse, and it can be worse than the shock felt upon arrival in the host country.

Because this reverse culture shock can be so painful and frustrating, it requires above all else sensitivity and deep caring on the part of those who minister. But you can help. You can make the difference for a missionary on furlough, or an MK in his first year of college. You can do it best through your own home. You *can* have a vital part in helping them to come to terms with themselves, their churches, and with life in America, to have truly satisfying and productive furloughs and then return to their respective fields refreshed and rejuvenated, ready to pick up the tasks God has given them.

Here's another fact you may find hard to believe. One of the biggest problems missionaries face when they get home is the green monster—yes, envy—the same one that comes to you on occasion to make you completely dissatisfied with what you have. Walking into an American home, with its lovely furnishings all clean and freshly scrubbed (even though it may not be at all), can be very unsettling, depending on what kind of home the missionary had on the field. During our first five years in Pakistan, we lived in a small town on the backside of the desert. Among the other missionaries near us, our town was known as the *S.A.S. Station—Suffering and Sacrifice*. Our house would not be called "adequate" in anyone's book. Actually, it didn't seem so bad to us after a while—that is, until we came home. Then the contrast was stark.

Now, I do not mean to imply that all missionaries live in shacks or lean-tos or grass huts. During our first term we soon realized we were fortunate to have a house at all. Finding houses in our small town was next to impossible. We had spent hours as a group of missionaries trying to define what was an "adequate house." You try that sometime with a group of your friends. Again, it's impossible simply because of the differences in people. What is adequate for one person isn't adequate for another. So much is involved and each person and each family comes at it from a different direction.

The thing that struck us more than anything was the settledness that pervades American homes. They seem so permanent—the way they are built, the way they are furnished, the way people live.

The fact that our work was in one of the hottest areas of Pakistan necessitated leaving our stations and going to the hills for the summer. Consequently, we never were settled. We would leave for the hills in May, taking the belongings we needed for the summer. Then at the end of the summer, the same process began all over again. All we did was pack, store, travel. Arriving back at the station we faced cleaning out termite dust, scrubbing the place down, unpacking and starting all over again. On and on it went.

Of course, we got used to it there. But on arrival back in America, the feeling of being vagabonds wandering to and fro on the face of the earth was accentuated by deputation, time spent traveling representing the mission. We were in a different bed and at a different table several times a week. The green monster did his work very effectively and it was easy to ask, "Why can't I have what these people have? Why can't I be settled in one place like they are?" Of course I realize now that people here aren't nearly as settled as they appear to be. Americans, too, are on the move.

So how can you use hallowed hospitality as you attempt to make the stay of these missionaries more normal, more relaxed and pleasant, and less traumatic? Here are a few suggestions.

When a missionary is coming to your church, don't wait for the pastor to plead, "Can't anyone entertain the missionaries while they are with us?" Don't wait to be asked. Get your bid in first, not because you feel guilty if you don't, but because you really want to. These missionaries need nothing more than to know that people want to be with them, that people are willing to take them off their pedestals and treat them as real, normal people—in short, that people will accept them for who and what they are. They don't want to be treated like artifacts in a museum. They want to be made to feel completely at home. They don't need or want to be fed in such a way that they get the impression you are fattening them for the kill. If you eat boxed pizzas, feed them boxed pizzas, too. And remember that weight control becomes extremely difficult when each night they are in a different home being treated like royalty.

It isn't a bad idea to ask if they have preferences in food, something they long for. Maybe they have had ham for the last six nights in a row, and are longing for a simple meal of scrambled eggs and bacon. How well I remember (my kids do, too) one particularly long stretch of deputation in an area where ham must have been on sale. We had ham every place we went. At the end of the long stretch, we were invited for Sunday dinner at the pastor's home. On the way there we were all wondering if it would be ham again, hoping it wouldn't. Upon our arrival, the pastor's little daughter ran all the way to the car to meet us, announcing, "We're having ham for dinner!" It was hard for us to conceal our disappointment, but it obviously was a treat for them, and we faced it with smiles and thanks.

And visiting missionaries don't care if the room you put them in overnight is fancy. They just like a place where they can unwind and spread out and be quiet. Some get used to being in a different bed every night. Others never do. It was never a problem for me because I can sleep anywhere. My husband is just the opposite. For him, deputation was hard, and he would opt for driving 300 miles home after an evening service so he could be in his own bed. In short, it can be a real struggle to get proper rest while on deputation. You can help with this problem by being sensitive to the needs of your missionary guest. Do all you can to offer them a private and quiet place.

Almost as severe as the strains of being in a different bed every night and eating too many sumptuous meals is endless conversation. Of course you want to get to know them and they in turn want to get to know you. They really do. But so often these occasions become a marathon of unending small talk and chatter, on and on, into the night. When you realize that this goes on night after night for the missionary, it is no wonder that conversation becomes a real pitfall of deputation. Just recently a missionary on furlough told me of one such experience. He was taken after the evening service to the home of his host. Then the visiting began, going on and on until midnight. He still had not been shown where he was to sleep, not even where the bathroom was. He related how as the minutes ticked by he was almost desperate, and his chatter was fast becoming that of a blithering idiot. His eyelids were unbelievably heavy. Finally, they showed him to his room, but by then he was too tired to sleep. He went to his next assignment, a Monday morning 7:00 breakfast with a group of pastors, feeling numb and weary and totally inadequate to speak to them.

Be sensitive to the needs of your missionary guest.

Missionaries usually like to be with children, but keep your children under control. Your own children will benefit greatly from having missionaries in the home, but don't let your children victimize them, turning your energetic kids loose on them. Teach your children how to ask intelligent questions. Show them on a map or globe where the missionary is from.

If you're going to be gone in the daytime, show your guest where everything is so he can spend a quiet day with his needs met while you are gone. If you have shopping centers and restaurants nearby, show him where they are. And be sure to give him a key to your home in case he wants to go out during the day.

If you find you are going to be gone from home for an extended period, why not give your pastor or your mission office a call and let them know that your home is available for house-sitting by a missionary or a missionary family? We did this once in California, and there are times even now when I dream of those two wonderful weeks in a lovely home in the hills of Southern California where we had time to recoup and gear up for the next stint of deputation. It was wonderful. It became a place of refuge, a place of quiet and serenity in the midst of a busy schedule. We could be ourselves and do whatever we wanted—relax, write, read, or entertain.

Now those, of course, are some obvious things. But we can go much further than this.

If you like sports—baseball, or football, basketball, track, soccer—or concerts, plays, art shows, craft shows, it doesn't matter. If the baseball game is Little League, church league, sandlot, high school, college or professional, or the concert is classical or something else, it doesn't matter. Chances are if you enjoy those things, the missionaries will too. If your own kids or friends are involved in any of these activities, invite the missionary to go along too. Last year my husband and I were entertaining in our home a missionary from Japan. We didn't know him at all, but since we are baseball fans, we invited him to go to a game with us. There was one problem: he was a Chicago fan, and we are Minnesota Twins fans. But did we have fun! He graciously became an overnight Twins fan (we didn't even threaten him about it). The evening was delightful for all of us. He told us it was exactly what he needed. He had been on a grueling deputation routine, day and night, and he needed to know there was life other than deputation.

A few years ago when we had a missionary couple with us, we noticed the Ice Capades were in town. We knew they needed relaxation more than they needed another heavy meal or evening of chatter. We took them to the Ice Capades and they loved it. In a few days we sent them on their way refreshed and relaxed.

Use picnics as a special time of ministry for missionaries. For us in Pakistan, a picnic consisted of trying to find a spot with a few blades of grass along a smelly, filthy canal. The picnic spots in America are quite unbelievable and they need to be used. Invite a missionary family or a single missionary to join you for a picnic in a park. You don't have to make a big production of it—you don't even have to grill anything. Pack a picnic basket (or cardboard box) with the kind of items your missionary might never get on the field, and then go out and relax in the outdoors. Add to your gear a softball bat and glove and ball, badminton rackets, a soccer ball, and determine that you will help him unwind and relax in the beauty and informality of the outdoors. It always seemed to me that true Christian conversation was enhanced in such a setting.

I have a friend in Southern California who has such a heart for missions that she decided to become a Mary Kay saleslady. She went through all the training, made the necessary investment, and began her new career. She promised the Lord that if He would help her in this, every cent of profit would go to missions. She kept her word and became very successful. Not only did she send sizable gifts to missions, but she made missionary ladies the focus of her expertise. I can never forget the evening she had my daughter and I come. She gave us complete facials, then sent us on our way with a full complement of Mary Kay products—gratis. This same lady and her husband were recently on a TV show and ended up winning $10,000. When we asked her son (a missionary in Colombia) if they were going to use the money to make a trip to Colombia, he replied, "You know my mother better than that—she has already given it all away to missions."

If your budget will allow, it is always fun to take a missionary family on a shopping tour, especially just after they have arrived home. I think this is one of the greatest dreads in coming home— how long will it take and how much money will be required to get us outfitted so that we look like normal human beings and not frumpy missionaries? They do worry about such things. You can adopt one child and commit yourself to outfitting that one child. Or you could take on the whole family—either by sewing or buying clothes. But, by all means, let them have a part in choosing what they will wear. You have heard, I am sure, some of the horror stories connected with missionary barrels. To sum it up, what these missionaries need to know is that there are people who understand a bit of the reverse culture shock they are going through. They want to know that you care about them and want to help in any way you can.

I could share much more—I'll just name a few. One fun activity is to get your missionary family involved in camping programs during the summer months. Recently a group of families from our church, who always spend their vacations at our church camp's Family Camp, invited our furloughing missionary couple to be their guests for a week at Family Camp. The church people pooled their resources and paid the whole fee. The missionaries were not scheduled to do any speaking—they just went along for the sheer joy of it. In this way the church people had an ideal opportunity over an extended period of time to get well acquainted with the missionary couple. We are all able to pray more intelligently for them, and we look forward to doing it again on their next furlough.

There are retreat centers now in a number of places in the U.S. that are designed to provide a refuge, a safe and serene place for people to come for rest. One such center has recently been opened in our own area by a couple who themselves have been missionaries. Their lovely retreat center is located on a beautiful river, nestled in the trees. The facilities are complete and often just what the doctor ordered. Several families in a church could pay the costs of sending a missionary family for a week at a place like this. They might prefer to go with someone else. There are places available, but oftentimes the cost makes it prohibitive for the missionary to arrange it himself.

The important thing is that each of us do what we can in our own creative ways to help these choice servants of the cross. What we have said about missionaries on furlough can also be said about those who are retiring from long lives on the mission field. This also can be a traumatic experience for them. We can do much to help these retirees. Many of them will have left all their earthly possessions on the fields—their household goods, books, linens—everything. They have to start all over again when they come home to retire. At this moment the women's group in our church is planning an appreciation night for one of our retiring missionaries. She will be moving to Arizona to start all over again. When we asked her what we could do in the way of a shower, she surprised us by telling us that she left all her Christian books for the library in the Bible School in Zaire. She came home with nothing but her Bible. She gave us a list of some of those books that she would really like to have replaced, and we are delighted to be able to have a part in meeting this need.

Use your imagination. Ask questions. Get acquainted with missionaries. Find out their special needs and then make a move to help meet them.

Let's move on to discuss missionary kids, that special breed of young people. I want to focus particularly on those who have left their families behind and have come home to work, study, or just to live. They find themselves in their "homeland," although for many it really isn't home at all. For some of them, the transition is easy and smooth. For others, it involves great pain and real suffering—severe culture shock in reverse. Some never seem to be able to adjust at all.

I think the kindest thing we can do for them is to not stereotype or generalize. Don't squish them all into one mold. There is a lot we can do to help them, but first of all it requires extreme sensitivity, compassion and much patience. Being involved in a Christian college where there are a large number of missionary kids, we are learning first of all what we can be to them, and *then* what we can do for them. During these 12 years we have learned a lot about them.

Because these kids experience such a wide range of reactions and experiences as they come home, it follows that each must be treated and ministered to uniquely. Some don't want to be bothered at all. Just leave them alone. That's what they want. But I believe this is the exception rather than the rule. On the whole, they are a group of kids who are bright, sharp, motivated, and very much in touch with the whole world. Often they are frustrated at the narrow vision of their counterparts in America, and they don't mind expressing it— at least to the right people. Many are fiercely independent, while others are pitifully dependent.

Some come with a lot of self-confidence and independence and poise and fit in with no problem at all. From this group, a large number easily assume positions of leadership. Most of these are very close to their parents and to the land in which they have grown up. From the moment of arrival, they begin to make plans to go "home" for a visit. But their anticipation is healthy and normal, and it does not interfere with their adjustment to life in the United States. They write their parents often, call often, keep in touch with other relatives, are neither proud nor ashamed of being MK's. They are normal, well-adjusted individuals.

Then there are those who seem to want to get lost in the woodwork. They aren't anxious for anyone to know they are MK's, or at least they don't want to be singled out as being unusual or different. Some of them express bitterness, especially if they have had bad experiences in boarding schools. Some don't want to be involved in anything to do with missions. As sponsors of our Student Missions Fellowship, we find it rare for an MK to be willing to take a position of leadership. Often we find MK's that seem to cling to other MK's, feeling they are the only ones who understand them.

For most of us, the best way to get acquainted with MK's is through the local church. Next best is through your mission agency. Once you have established contact with one or several, invite them to your home. Make them feel at home, and as soon as you can do it with sensitivity and wisdom, let them know that you would like them to consider your home their home away from home. Some will latch on to the invitation immediately. With others you will have to go slowly and prove to them that you want them to be a part of your family. Each has to be dealt with in his own way.

If you want to have fun, and have a real lesson in the psychology of MK's, invite a bunch of college MK's for a Sunday dinner. One such occasion at our house stands out in my mind. I fixed a huge pot of chicken curry—and a bigger pot of rice. I made Pakistani bread, which takes hours and hours. I invited eight missionary kids—most from Africa, but a few from the Orient. Believe me, it was an interesting, hilarious sociological study. I was amazed (although I shouldn't have been) as they discussed all the spots on the globe where they had been. They talked and laughed about their experiences in airports (in exotic places such as Abu Dhabi!), problems with visas, experiences in MK schools, hair-raising experiences in jungles. Most important were not the stories but the camaraderie among these eight kids. They had so much in common, and as soon as they began to let down their guard, they were at home with one another.

My advice for ministry to these kids is first of all to be extremely watchful of their feelings. You can't push yourself—you can't make them fit into any mold at all. Be very patient, and don't give up on the first rebuff. Call your nearest Christian college, or get in touch with your mission agency to see if there are any MK's in your area. Reach out cautiously and carefully. You might be surprised at the outcome. It will be a blessing to your family, and it could end up being just what an MK needs during his time in the U.S. without his parents.

We recently entertained an MK in our home for the last weekend of a long school break. We took to each other immediately. We took her everywhere with us. We let her spend time quietly in her room. We encouraged her to play the piano. She wrote letters, played, shopped, did her homework, read, and helped in the kitchen. She was so easy to have around, and she knew she was welcome at any time. She had no sooner left than I got a call for suggestions for a speaker at a women's meeting. The Lord reminded me of this young lady, who could do a good job presenting to these women the life of an MK. She ended up going to speak for these women, and she did a terrific job. In the meantime, we were able to help her get two more speaking engagements. Through our befriending her, we had a part in making American Christians more cognizant of what life as an MK is like, and I have no doubt that it contributed to more intelligent prayer for missionary kids.

I have written much about missionaries. Perhaps that is because missions is a high priority in our lives, that which is closest to our hearts. But we should expand a bit and include the special ministries we can have to God's prophets and ministers of all kinds.

Have you ever wondered what went on in the home of Mary and Martha and Lazarus when they got word that Jesus was coming to visit them? After all, this was not just an ordinary guest—this was Jesus, their Lord and Master. We need to stop and think of how important the whole practice of hospitality was in those days. There weren't motels and hotels. Inns were notoriously filthy, both morally and physically. It was absolutely necessary for the followers of Jesus to practice hospitality in the entertaining of Jesus and His disciples as they wandered around the country. It must have been very exciting for these people to entertain the "dignitaries" of this new religion sweeping the land. It ought to be exciting for us, too.

How well I remember the stream of visiting ministers, missionaries, and evangelists who came to our home. It was exciting and my mother had a knack of making us realize what a privilege it was. Although we didn't have a separate apartment in our home, we were very pleased to be able to "give up our rooms" for visiting ministers and missionaries.

I am sure you would be surprised to know that in our day and age it is not an easy job finding a place for a visiting missionary to stay overnight. That may sound strange, but it is true. In my work of scheduling and arranging for visits of missionaries to churches, I have often found that it is like pulling teeth trying to find places for them to stay. This is more true in the large city churches than in rural areas, but I am sorry to say it is very true.

On the other hand, there are a number of places I can call at any time knowing that at a moment's notice the welcome mat will be out to any visiting missionary who comes along. I have always loved the story of the Shunammite woman who was so concerned that the prophet Elisha have a place where he could rest and relax that she fixed up a special room for him on her rooftop. Challenged by this example, many churches have set up a place which they call their "prophet's chamber." Some people have done the same in their homes. It is indeed a beautiful custom. It might be that you have a quiet spot in your home which could become a haven of rest for a weary servant of God.

I believe that some people within the Body of Christ have the ability and the personality to have a special ministry with these servants of God. I am not saying it is always easy. I would also add that they aren't always good guests; nevertheless they are God's special messengers. Hospitality is to be extended to them as well, and God has promised special blessings to those who engage in this type of entertaining.

Probably one of the best examples of this type of hospitality in the New Testament is found in III John. Gaius is commended in this tiny book because he cared for his fellow workers in the Gospel. The fact that he is mentioned and commended for this leads us to believe that he looked upon it as something special he could do. It's also interesting that his wife, if he had one, isn't mentioned at all. Gaius looked upon this ministry as the Christian's duty and he evidently carried it out with finesse and grace.

Like Gaius, we must keep our homes and purses open for the care of God's prophets. It is not only our duty but it is our rich privilege. Perhaps you do not feel called into this kind of Christian service yourself, as God may not have called you to be a missionary. But we can all be active participants in missions and ministry by keeping our hearts open to serve God through our homes, and by compassionate service to those who have been called.

Chapter Ten

When It's Our Turn to Receive

During our first years of ministry as missionaries in Pakistan, we spent our summers in the foothills of the Himalayas doing language study in the national language of Pakistan, Urdu. It is a very old language, a mixture of many languages. Actually the word itself means "camp"—the idea being that it is a language which has borrowed from other languages close to it.

We learned to hear and understand, to speak (although haltingly and very simply), and to read and to write. We were both full-time students those summers, juggling our responsibilities as parents with the demands of language study. Along with attending classes in the morning, we each studied with a private tutor in the afternoon. In between we practiced what we had learned. It took raw courage. To suddenly be reduced to speaking like a child when you're 30 is a humbling experience.

Urdu is a language with a rich literary history. Asian countries have a long tradition of stories and proverbs handed down through the ages that are known to everyone.

Our first reading primer contained a very old Pakistani story, "Guest and Host." I can remember vividly the first time we stumbled through it and were able to translate it. It epitomizes in story form what hospitality in that culture is all about. It tells of the demands made upon a host as he practices his own religion through hospitality. It speaks of entertaining friends, relatives, strangers, travelers, even enemies. It is a beautiful glimpse into the culture, and portrays the religious overtones of the practice of hospitality.

Along with the responsibilities of hosts, there is a section dealing with what it means to be a guest—a good guest. And perhaps we need to digress a bit and look at the subject from the other side of the coin. I hope we have learned what is involved in being a gracious host. Now let us say a few words about what is involved in being a good guest, for they go together.

When I think of the qualities found in a good guest, I cannot help thinking of experiences where people entertained in my childhood were not good guests at all. We would have found it hard to say this Irish rhyme to them:

> Come in the evening, come in the morning;
> Come when expected, come without warning.
> Thousands of welcomes you'll find here before you,
> And the oftener you come, the more we'll adore you.

In our experiences, many have come when expected, albeit some have come quite late. Often it is unavoidable and therefore forgivable. I believe as many arrived in the middle of the night as in the evening or morning. We got used to it.

The ones who have come without warning often haven't had a way to let us know. On the other hand, many could have let us know—and they should have. I can honestly say that for almost all who came to our home to sit at our table, to sleep in our beds, we usually could and did give them a thousand welcomes. We had tasted the joys of hospitality and so we gladly shared our home. But there were some to whom it was almost impossible to say (although we said it anyway), "The oftener you come, the more we'll adore you." To put it bluntly, they were miserable guests.

I am not suggesting that my guests conform exactly to what I expect of them. I really do want a guest to feel free, at home, and relaxed in my home. But there are some simple and basic courtesies that can make any of us a better guest—indeed, a welcome guest.

In our discussion of the Christian home as a means of blessing and ministry to others, we can lay down some simple principles for guests. I trust we all will have that privilege from time to time, even though we may find ourselves actually doing more entertaining than being entertained.

I first suggest that a good guest will do his utmost to be at the home of his host at the appointed time. If you aren't sure about the time, then ask. Maybe the time has not been exactly set. Sam thinks it strange that sometimes I tell people to come between 6:00 and 6:30—he believes in being more specific than that. The fact is, sometimes that half-hour period is definite enough—it really doesn't make that much difference. As the guest, you should try very hard to fit into that time frame. And if for some reason you can't, do your host the simple courtesy of giving them a call to let them know you will be late (that is, assuming that you are in a place where a phone call can be made). It can often mean the difference between a properly cooked meal and a burnt sacrifice. It is easy to be courteous. It can even be habit-forming, but it takes that extra bit of effort.

Another mark of a good guest is the ability to know when enough is enough. It is better to leave the home of your host while they are still enjoying you than to go one minute too long. The "please stay" can change to the unspoken "please go" in one split second. It's better to leave while you are still enjoying yourself than to stay one moment too long. Again it is a simple matter of reading other people and being courteous.

If you are in another person's home with your own children, courtesy demands that you keep your own children in line. Don't make your host do it. Never discipline another person's child—never, never. Again, a crash course for your child is not enough. It's too late once you get there. Make your child understand what you expect of him while he is a guest. You will be much more apt to be invited back. I hate to say this, but there are some people I invite to my home with dread. Not that my home is so special or so much in order. It is just that my friends' children make it difficult for everyone. A little control and discipline would help the situation immensely.

As I write this, a picture from years ago pops into my head. I was a student in seminary and living with my sister and her husband. My sister was ill at the time, and it was my responsibility to do the cleaning and cooking. They had friends who had the strange habit of coming on a social call on Saturday mornings. Maybe that doesn't seem like a strange time to you, but it does to me, especially when each visit was unannounced. They had one little boy who was a terror, a pistol, a bombshell. He was gorgeous—and he was awful. It took one visit from this family to teach me what had to be done. When I saw them drive up, I immediately started swooping up breakable things from the living room. I ran around battening down the hatches. Anything moveable and breakable, I stashed away in a closet. That kid was a royal pain in the neck. I dreaded to see him come. And how I wished his parents would have seen that their precious little child absolutely ruined our visits. I don't hold it against the boy as much as his parents. They chose not to see or respond to what he was doing. Conversation was all but impossible and it took more than one pair of eyes to keep the little guy under constant surveillance. He probably grew up to be a fine young man, and by this time I am sure he has tasted the joys of being a parent. I wish I could remember him with more fondness. As far as I am concerned, these people were not good guests. Good people, but not good guests.

I don't know what Gloria Vanderbilt or Emily Post would say about the practice of bringing gifts when you are a guest. I think there is no hard and fast rule. I believe the practice of bringing gifts can easily become an expense and a chore, and it can also produce embarrassment for the host. But if you have never tried it, I would suggest that you try it once. It is fun from the giving standpoint. I love the European custom of bringing fresh flowers when you are invited to someone's home, and even bringing one flower shows you have gone to extra effort. In Minnesota, the cost of flowers is prohibitive, but I can afford one long-stemmed carnation or daffodil or even a rose. Or try bringing a bouquet from your own garden. A small box of candy is always appropriate. There are many special little books and knick-knacks available that can often be icing on the cake for the host and hostess.

Thank you notes are always proper—not always essential, but surely always proper. Even with the high cost of postage, it is a beautiful custom that puts the finishing touch on a hospitality occasion. Again, it can be habit-forming, but it is a good habit to get into. It needn't be much—a few words of appreciation and expression of your joy at being a guest. It really isn't hard to write a thank you note. It takes only a bit of effort, and often it can spur a host and hostess on to doing more entertaining.

In informal entertaining, I feel it is always proper for the guests to at least suggest that they help with the cleanup.

May I give a special word of encouragement to husbands at this point. Do you realize what a good testimony and fine example it is when the husband, not just the wife, is quick to offer assistance to a non-Christian host or hostess when the time comes for cleanup? Often such an offer of help, in another person's home, is a vivid demonstration of a loving and caring spirit which only Christ can give. After all, our relationship to Christ ought to make us the *most* sensitive and caring people in the world. I heard of one instance where this happened. The hostess asked the wife of the guest who offered to help if he had *always* been like this. It was a good opportunity for this woman to share with her non-Christian friend how Jesus had changed her husband.

Our cultural waters in America these days are very muddy. Sometimes, with all the controversy raging about women's place, women's lib, and all the rest, a man doesn't know where he is supposed to fit in. I think it is quite safe to say that Christian men should have the same servant heart that Christ himself had. If it was proper for Jesus to serve, why isn't it just as proper for men today to serve? You see, when Jesus comes into a life, He changes us—He really does. He changes those of us who are women, and He changes men, too. The man no longer has to lord it over a woman, expecting always to be served. We must all become servants.

We need fine-tuned sensitivity in this, realizing that things are changing so fast. We do not have to conform completely to our culture. It is still more important to be in tune with the precepts of God's Word and what it has done in our lives than to be dictated to by our culture. But one thing is sure. Non-Christians need to be able to *see* that we are different because of our personal relationship with Jesus Christ. We need to demonstrate to the world, to non-Christians, that in God's eyes we *are* all equal. Our gender isn't what is important—our relationship to Christ and His effect on our hearts and lives is what really matters. Such a knowledge should not only transform our relationships to one another, but also energize and vitalize our service to God. Scripture does not teach that women are to be the prime examples of loving service. If we need that example, it is surely our Lord himself, with a basin of water in one hand and towel over His shoulder, making the rounds of the upper room the night before He was crucified. This example is for both men and women.

Chapter Eleven

Having a Servant Heart

What better way to summarize all we have said about the total ministry of Christian hospitality than by looking again at the supreme example, Jesus Christ. This is nowhere more beautifully illustrated than in the account of the last supper He had with His disciples. John 13 records it like this (NIV): "It was just before the Passover Feast. Jesus knew that His time had come for him to leave this world and go to the Father. Having loved His own who were in the world, *He now showed them the full extent of His love.*" It was in the setting of a meal together with those He loved that He demonstrated what His love was really all about—serving. How very appropriate that at this crucial time in His life, He wanted more than anything to be with those He loved. He not only wanted to be with them, but also to show them the extent of His servanthood.

To me the conclusion is very clear. We have looked at the excuses we use to avoid practicing hospitality, the problems, the pitfalls, the methods, and the special groups of people who are to be the recipients of our service.

But we must go back to the matter of the attitudes and principles that should be present in our practice of hospitality. Without them our serving becomes nothing more than a duty, sometimes a drudgery, a meaningless activity we go through. Right attitudes can transform our efforts from drudgery and nervous activity to peace, tranquillity, deep satisfaction, and the knowledge that hospitality is indeed a service which we render to God. What, then, are these attitudes?

Have the heart of a servant. Being a willing servant is the beginning of Christian hospitality. As Christ came to serve, so must we live our lives in total service to God and to others. In the area of hospitality, the servant's heart will be manifested as we open our homes without expecting anything in return. Christian hospitality does not keep accounts of who had who over last.

Be very careful about being too busy to serve. We must not allow ourselves the luxury of using this threadbare excuse. Each of us has twenty-four hours in a day; each of us has time to do something. Our willingness is bound up in our desire to do something for people. It diminishes the fetish of a clean house. No one can keep the goal of an immaculate house perfectly all the time. Don't let the clean house syndrome get in the way. People are always more important.

Get rid of the lame excuses that come so easily. Whether it be our time, budget, living situation, or our lack of know-how, it's best not to make a habit of using excuses. Do away with them once for all.

Always have enough to share. Hospitality must be looked at as sharing of what we have, not what we don't have, or we would like to have. Remember that hospitality can be as simple as a cup of coffee and a storebought cookie. Really.

Don't be intimidated and discouraged by interruptions. A true servant will always be able to suffer interruptions because that means time with people, not things.

Give a warm welcome. It is the beginning of gracious hospitality. Part of the definition of hospitality is "gladly received, as one whose coming gives pleasure." The initial greeting is so important—a warm smile, a hearty handshake, announcing our guests' presence to others in the family.

Learn to put guests at ease immediately. The first few moments are crucial. If this can best be done by having little puzzles, knickknacks, curios, special books, then use them.

Make guests know that we are honored by their presence. We can do this as we are free and relaxed with them. Be interested in the guests and their interests. Make them realize that their presence in our home is our honor.

Plan ahead—plan ahead. If everything is left until after our guests arrive, they will think their coming wasn't important enough to require some planning by the host. A little forethought can make a big difference to the atmosphere we create for our guests.

Remember that our hospitality will help us achieve the goals of becoming more effective in our evangelism and in building up one another in the Body of Christ.

In summary, we must remember that we should always put people above things, their needs above our convenience.

Since hospitality—true hallowed hospitality—begins with an attitude, then springs into action, we can best develop this spiritual gift by using Scripture as our example. As we bring our gifts and hospitality into loving commitment to God, who himself reached out to us in love and welcome, our gifts and efforts will be for His glory.

Chapter Twelve

A Finishing Touch

I am thankful it is not a mortal sin not to do everything according to tradition. It is permissible, even commendable, to adapt and innovate. Sometimes we might discard cherished traditions too easily, but it is wonderful to be free. On the other hand, it is also a good thing to cling to some time-honored ways of doing things.

Each of us carries with us as a part of our cultural baggage a sizeable number of traditions. Some are family heritage, some are national heritage. Some of them we do without even thinking—others we undertake in full consciousness that we are carrying on a cherished tradition.

In hospitality—setting our tables, serving food, setting times for entertaining—we all make conscious decisions whether to do things the way we have always done them or be creative enough to swerve from the ways (sometimes called the ruts) we find ourselves in.

Only you can decide whether you are free to do what is best for you in terms of your budget, time, home, personality and family situation. Be as free as you can without violating your own personality. The results will be amazing.

Some might not be aware of the various table services or the myriad ways of serving one can use. So it probably isn't superfluous to run through a few different modes of entertaining. It might help in deciding where to begin. It might also assist in preparation and planning, certainly in helping to pull it off once the guests have arrived.

Fortunately, there are generally accepted guidelines to help us

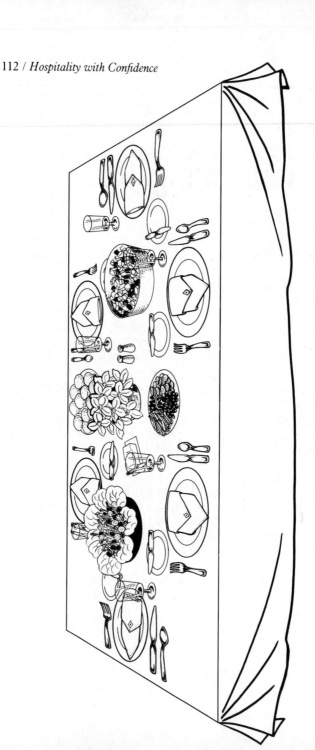

do what is considered proper in our society. This list is by no means exhaustive, but it gives ideas of the many alternatives you can use in your entertaining.

Country Style Service

Except for occasional buffet dinners (which I use when I have more people than I can seat at my table), country style service is what I do most. It was traditional in my home when I was growing up. I prefer it when I want to serve large groups of people (as many as I can seat at my table) in a short time and in a homey atmosphere. It does require a table big enough to hold all the serving dishes as well as seat the guests.

In this style, the table is completely set before guests sit down, and serving dishes are placed at intervals around the table so they can be easily passed. To avoid traffic jams, dishes of food should be passed in the same direction. Although there is probably no set order for the dishes to be passed around, I do have one small preference. If my meal includes gravy, I always try to see that the gravy follows immediately after the meat and potatoes. (Of course I realize that for our British friends, the gravy goes on *everything* and therefore should go around last!) If the table seems too crowded with all the serving dishes, you can always have a tea cart or a small table accessible to the hostess where the serving dishes can be placed after they have gone around.

Who waits on the table? Mother. But one or more other family members or even a guest can help remove the main course dishes. I suggest removing all the serving dishes, including butter, jam, condiments, before serving dessert. Of course, this is also my personal preference.

Family Service

Family service differs from country style in that the family members actually help serve the food. Usually two people at opposite ends of the table dish up individual portions and pass the plate to each person until all have been served. This style is ideal for serving casseroles which come directly from the oven and are too hot to pass. You can use just one person (perhaps the host or hostess) to serve the casserole, passing the plate to each person, then passing the rest of the food. Or you can serve everything on the plate before it is passed to the guest. If you have guests you feel at ease with, you can ask the person on the server's left to help serve the food.

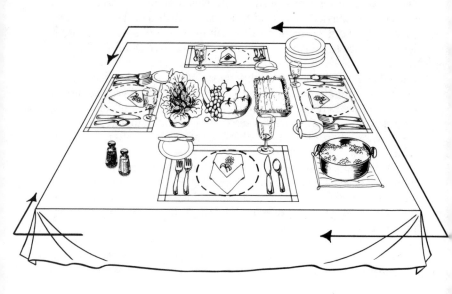

Apartment Service

This style is especially useful when the house is small, particularly when there is no dining room. Food is dished up in the kitchen and carried to the eating area. The method is also good when there are small children—each child gets a portion of everything and there isn't the danger of spilled food, to say nothing of arguments about whether the child wants what he sees. This style is sometimes called "blueplate service."

Apartment service works best with a small number of people as too many guests would require too much time in the kitchen serving the plates. The food may actually be dished up on plates just before guests sit down, making it possible to get the meal moving in a hurry. It is easy to clear the table before the dessert course and the whole thing can be carried out with a minimum of fuss.

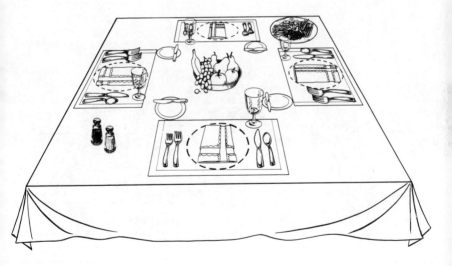

Buffet Service

Buffet service is by far the most convenient way to entertain large groups of people. But there are precautions you need to take. If people are going to end up standing while they eat, eliminate anything that requires a knife. Unfortunately, we are born with only two hands and it is difficult to handle too many implements at the same time. It is easiest to have the silverware rolled into a napkin or inserted into a napkin folded diagonally to produce a pocket.

An advantage of this mode is that the meal can be served not only from a table, but from a kitchen counter, buffet, desk, or chest. If you have card tables or other smaller tables, you can set them with everything except the plate so people can fill their plates and then be seated. If you don't have a place to set them at a table, it is good to supply trays. Also, be sure to have a place for people to set their drinks. If you are worried about polished surfaces of your tables, be sure to provide coasters.

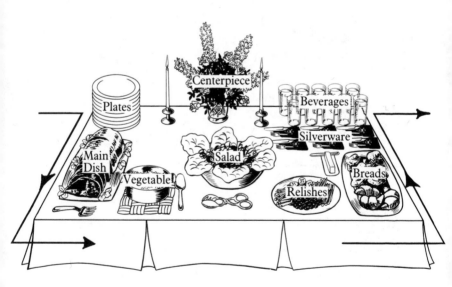

Come for Tea Style

This is an easy, inexpensive way to entertain. It provides an air of graciousness that I love. It can be used for a few close friends or a larger group. Times can vary—after church, afternoon, morning, late at night. Almost any kind of table can be used. The Norwegians have developed this to a fine art, and the British, of course, are the real professionals. It is versatile, and for any size group the menu is basically the same—tea (or coffee or both) and a few dainty foods, sweet and/or savory to nibble on. One of the greatest advantages is that it allows unhurried, unharried time for everyone.

Informal tea for a few guests should be served in the living room where everyone can sit down. Fill the cups with tea and offer them cream and sugar, which you have available, but let the guests help themselves to the food.

Formal tea for a larger group is a stand-up affair. Guests get their refreshments from the dining room then move into the living room. At this kind of tea it is especially nice to have one person to pour coffee and tea and another, punch.

You can decide whether you want to leave your table bare or use a small tablecloth on your tea table. Use either cloth napkins or small paper tea napkins. If you have never entertained before, give this a try.

I hope you gleaned enough from the chapters of this book to realize I don't advocate your going out and buying expensive china and crystal and flatware so you can get started in entertaining. I feel strongly about using what we have, starting where we are, and most of all bringing all our creative energies to bear. Most importantly, we must get started. It is not necessary to own china. It isn't even necessary to have matching sets of dishes—in fact, no law says you can't use paper plates or at least the new "chinette" types. And surely you don't need to have more than one set of dishes. What you have now in your kitchen will work for anything. If you don't feel at ease with formal entertaining, then don't do it. Find something you are comfortable with.

So let's move on to discuss table service and table settings, starting with a few comments about centerpieces, candles and table linens. You may have a trunkful of linens you received as wedding gifts or that were passed on to you from your mother. Maybe you've never used them because you hate to wash and iron. Or you may have placemat and napkin sets still in their original boxes. I challenge you to use these items. Don't let them rot and yellow in the chest or cupboard.

Entertaining is not just the food served, but the way it's served. Each time you set your table, it demonstrates your own creativity— or lack of it. The appearance of the table is important both to you and your guests. The theme of the occasion can be cast by the way we set our table. It shows our guests that we care. It is exciting to express our own taste and flair. Whether we use china or paper plates, plastic flatwear or sterling silver, paper placemats or linen tablecloths, or paper or cloth napkins, our tables can be a work of art.

Whatever you do, use color. Though color is extremely important, it doesn't mean everything has to match perfectly. If you use your mother's beautiful white linen tablecloth, and your china is also white (like mine), bring color to your table with candles, flowers, and colored napkins. If you use placemats, they don't all have to be the same color, nor do napkins. With the blending of many colors, a table can be made to look like a gorgeous country garden. Don't be afraid to use stripes, checks, prints, polka dots, mixing them with plain colors.

As for dinnerware, if you have a set that includes only dinner plates, cups, and saucers, never mind. That really is enough. You could travel the garage sale circuit and perhaps find clear glass salad plates that go with anything. Use what you have. Don't ever be guilty of using your lack of complete dinnerware as an excuse.

For glassware, a tumbler is sufficient for anything. You don't have to have crystal goblets, but if you do, use them once in a while, though probably not when small children are at the table. The same is true for dessert dishes. Nothing is wrong with using a variety of dishes to serve dessert.

Further, nothing says we have to have more than one set of flatware. Today's stainless steel is so elegant and sturdy that it can be used for both formal and informal entertaining. If you are buying flatware, keep in mind the constant need for extra teaspoons. If you use iced-tea spoons, they don't have to match the rest of your set.

If by chance you have become famous for serving soup, you will need a basic set of soup bowls (not too big). I also recommend a real soup tureen with lid for serving and keeping the soup hot.

Baskets are popular and appropriate on any kind of table. They can be holders for casserole dishes, buns and breads, and some desserts.

For a special touch of beauty and romance on the table, I use candles. My sister often serves leftovers (which she calls a "must-go" meal) by candlelight, transforming the occasion from the mundane to something special. But there are some things to remember about candles. The flame should be either below or above eye level. The reason is obvious: you don't want your guests to leave the table with impaired vision! Extra long candles can be put in low holders and short candles in tall holders. Or you can use an arrangement of a group of candles of varying lengths, as long as each is above or below eye level. Again, colors can be varied and should be coordinated with linens and dinnerware. White is always appropriate for candles, and these can be enhanced by dainty silk flower rings. You don't have to have a lot of candles—just one or two sets—and candle rings of varying colors to change the mood.

Centerpieces can be a touch of charm, elegance, or drama to transform a dull table into something extraordinary. Use what you have—cut crystal, ceramic, glass, silver, wood, straw. Use silk flowers, real flowers, or even potted plants, which can be jazzed up with a bright candle or a bright ribbon.

If you go for tall, full, soaring arrangements, be sure they are set firmly in place so they don't tip over. And remember, no matter how dramatic your centerpiece may seem to you, if it is too high for one of your seated guests to see over, it will inhibit easy conversation and will become an obstacle to communication.

Small, delightful touches can be created with miniature table decorations. You can take containers like glass salt dishes (I inherited mine from my mother) and put a flower in each one. Or you can buy in Scandinavian stores metal clip-on candle holders that can be clipped to the dinner or salad plate. Coordinate the tiny colored candle with the centerpiece or center candles. It makes a lovely effect.

Check through your cupboards for unusual objects to use for centerpieces. Wooden shoes, baskets, toothpick holders, brass knick-knacks can all be used with flair. There is no end to what you can do to make your table look beautifully elegant.

I am a tablecloth user. I realize many people feel as strongly about avoiding real linens in their entertaining as I do about using them. I don't mind washing and ironing. I even go out and buy new tablecloths when I see them on sale.

What can I say if you steadfastly refuse to use anything on your table except plastic placemats that can be wiped clean with a cloth? You are missing a lot. If you are willing to consider using linens, don't be afraid of color. Don't be afraid to mix solids and prints and patterns. Don't shy away from the gorgeous plaids. Try using quilt tops, rugs, bedspreads, cut fabrics. Just be creative and colorful.

I recently stumbled on a wonderful tablecloth sale. I broke down and bought four—one white and the rest colored. Rather than investing in cloth napkins, we went to a local wholesale paper products store and bought large dinner napkins in an array of colors that could be mixed and matched with the tablecloths. I also have a number of sets of candles and candle rings easily coordinated with the tablecloths and napkins. The results are amazing, not to mention the fun I have creating exactly the effect I want.

A word of caution: check the fabric content. Many newer, easy-care fabrics that are supposed to be so easy to care for are not. Spots caused by greasy foods such as spaghetti and barbecue sauce are impossible to get out. The lovely Scandinavian woven fabrics are beautiful and very easy to take care of. If carefully washed and dried, they don't need ironing at all.

Lace is easy to use, seldom requiring ironing. I like to use lace with colored liners (colored sheets work fine), coordinating the color with the center-piece.

There are no hard and fast rules about the shape of tablecloths. A good rule to follow, however, is that there should be an overhang of 12 to 16 inches, although that isn't absolutely necessary. The longer the overhang, the more formal your table becomes. If you have an oblong table, don't hesitate to use a rectanglular cloth, being sure to leave enough overhang. It is a bit harder to use an oblong cloth on a rectangular table,. but if the cloth is large enough, even that will work. Depending on the surface of your table, it is probably best to use a table pad, but if your tablecloth is heavy, it won't be necessary.

Another beautiful effect on a large table is a long runner down the middle, using placemats at each place. Again, mix and match adds the finishing touch.

Have you ever wondered how to give your plain and ordinary table setting a bit of dramatic flair to capture your guest's attention? The food, table setting, centerpiece and colors may all be just right, but you want that last finishing touch to set it apart.

Well, attractively folded table napkins can give your table a special look. I'm one who loudly declares, "I just can't do that type of thing with my hands!" I can type, play the piano, and do many other things, but I find it difficult to make my fingers cooperate when I fold napkins. Maybe we can motivate each other to move from the simple one-fold napkin to something creative and unexpected. I am willing to try and I hope you are, too.

Remember, napkins not only come in different fabrics but in different sizes and shapes. This is true both for cloth and paper napkins. Dinner napkins are usually 18″ to 24″. Luncheon napkins are a size smaller, or about 16″ in size. Tea napkins are 12″, and cocktail napkins are 4″. Napkins come in square or rectangular shapes.

Napkin folding styles vary from simple to quite complicated. Some are especially suited to buffet-type suppers and others to formal dinners. I have included a few basic ones for you to try. Take a handful of dinner napkins and practice. Discover which ones you like and are comfortable doing.

Where you place the napkin on your dinner, buffet, or tea table can be determined by the fold you use. Don't be afraid to experiment. Placement will also be dictated by the size of the table, the number of dishes on the table, and the type of flower arrangement. Don't be content with just folding a napkin in the usual rectangle. Be creative enough to try something different.

Buffet Fold

The Buffet Fold provides an attractive and simple means for guests to hold their plates, napkins and silverware comfortably. Both variations of this fold form a pocket in which to place silverware. Your buffet setting will appear elegant and well-organized. With either of these folds, do not use a napkin with a one-sided print.

Dinner Pocket Buffet Fold

1. Fold napkin in half.
2. Fold in half again with open corners at the top.
3. Fold the top corner, only, down.
4. Fold the corners behind the napkin.
5. There now is a pocket for silverware.

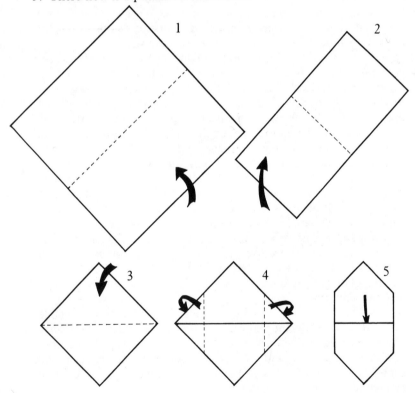

Diagonal Buffet Fold

1. Fold napkin in half.
2. Fold in half again with open corners at the top right.
3. Fold down upper right corner to the center.
4. Fold the same corner down twice more to form a diagonal pocket.
5. Fold down a second corner and tuck it into the pocket.
6. Fold each edge under (about ¼ of width each).
7. Place silverware in the pocket.

Variations: Use two paper napkins of different colors and fold as one. Or use for a dinner party and tuck place card upright between the two diagonal folds.

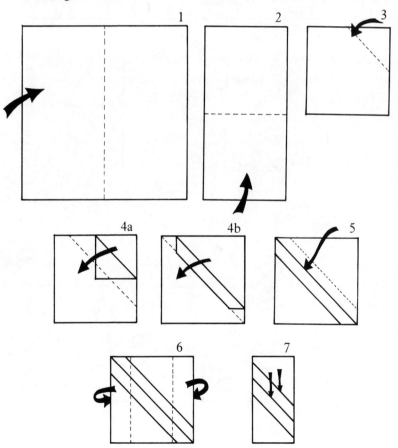

Dinner Fold

The Dinner Fold creates an elegant and formal appearance. This is an especially attractive way to highlight a decorative corner and edging on your napkin.

1. Fold any square napkin in half.
2. Fold in half again.
3. Rotate as shown.
4. Fold bottom up at a crease made just under the middle line.
5. Turn napkin over and fold one edge back.
6. Fold the other edge back and tuck into the pocket of the first edge.
7. Turn over.

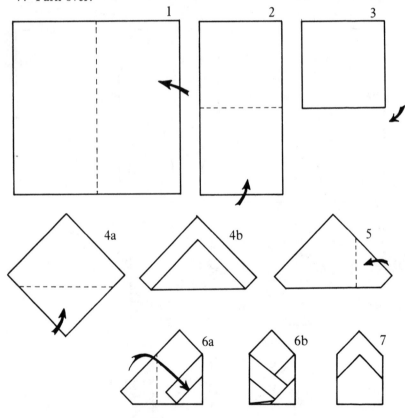

Fan in Napkin Ring

1. Choose a large dinner napkin. Fold the open napkin in half and crease.
2. Fold in half again length-wise and crease.
3. Starting on the left, make small accordian pleats of uniform size and crease firmly.
4. Tuck the bottom of the pleats into a napkin ring and fan out the top. Place fan on plate or just ahead of the fork.

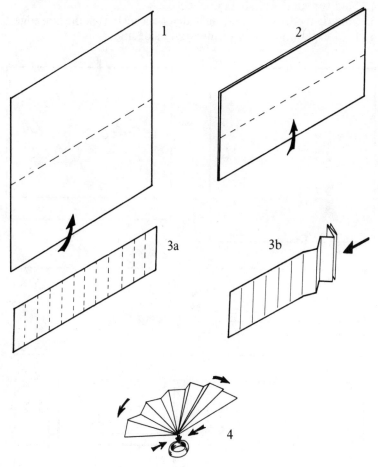

Openwork Fold

The Openwork Fold adds an elegant touch to your dinner table and is simple to learn.

Choose a square, one color napkin with a decorative edge and contrasting design.

1. Fold bottom edge up about ¼ of the height of the napkin.
2. Fold top edge down to about 1-1½″ from bottom fold edge.
3. Turn napkin over.
4. Fold left edge over about one inch.
5. Fold right edge over, placing it about one inch from the first edge.
6. Fold napkin in half by turning right side under.

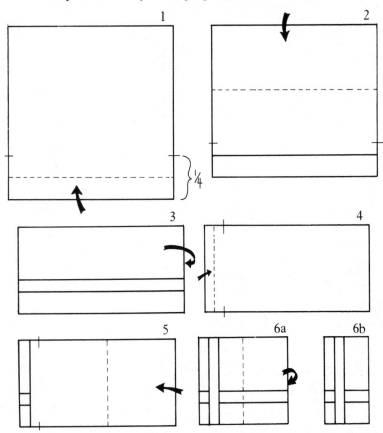

Cascade Fold

Choose a square napkin, either a solid color or with a woven print. A one-sided print will not work. Also choose a size appropriate to the dinner or luncheon plate on which it will be placed.

1. Fold napkin in half as shown.
2. Fold in half again as shown.
3. With open corners facing down, fold the first corner up to just below the top point.
4. Repeat with the three other corners staggering them as shown.
5. Fold last corner back down to the base line.
6. Fold edges back behind the napkin.
7. For an added touch, tuck a party favor or place card in the top fold of the napkin.

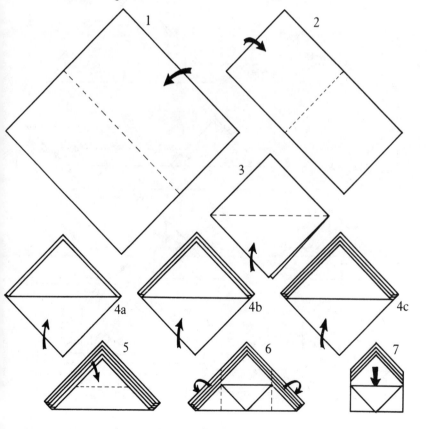

Flower Fold

This fold requires a large square napkin and a goblet in which to place the napkin. The deeper the goblet, the larger the napkin should be. Choose any square napkin, print or solid color.

1. Fold napkin into a triangle.
2. Fold bottom edge up about ⅓ of the height.
3. Fold napkin in half along the dotted line.
4. Starting in the center, make accordian pleats of uniform size on each side.
5. When one side is done, flip over and do the other side.
6. Place napkin in goblet, fanning out the pleats. Pull the ends down over the sides of the goblet to produce a flower effect.

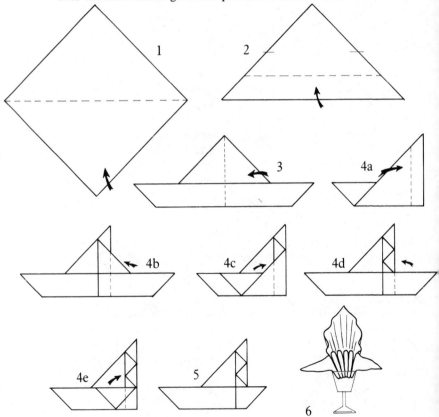

Blossom

1. Choose a large cloth or paper napkin. With napkin open, pick up the center and shake, allowing the folds to fall evenly.
2. Place folded end through a cup handle, between the prongs of a fork or tuck under the plate. (If napkin needs more bulk, fold the tip in half.)

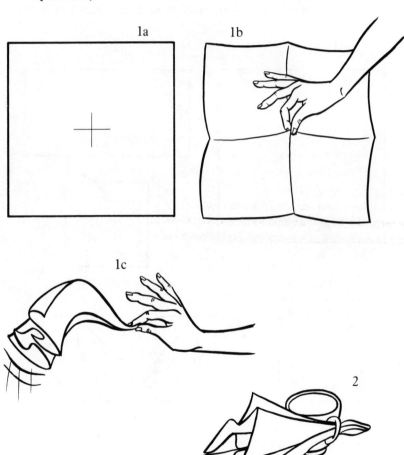

Triangle Fold

1. Fold a square napkin in half as shown.
2. Fold in half again. Open edges should be on the top right.
3. Fold top right corner back down to bottom left.
4. Fold this bottom left corner back up to the middle and the next top right corner down to the middle.
5. Fold the other two corners under to meet in the middle of the back.

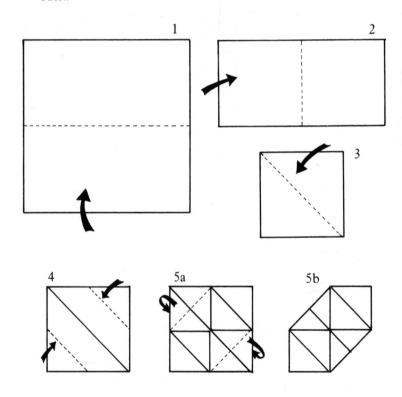

Center Fold

1. Fold a square napkin in half.
2. Fold in half again.
3. Fold bottom two corners up to meet in the middle.
4. Insert a flower or party favor into the fold.

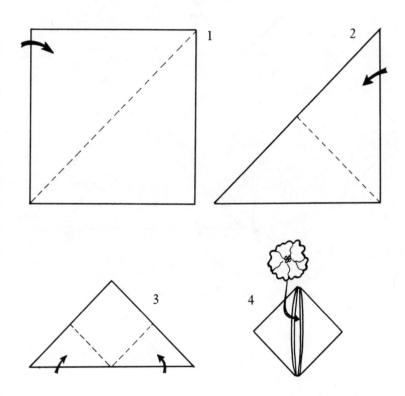

Kite Fold

1. Fold a square napkin in half as shown.
2. Fold both bottom corners up until they meet in the middle.
3. Fold outside corners again to meet in the middle.

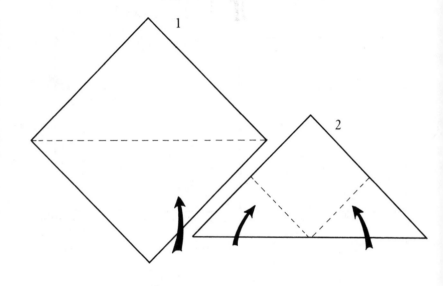

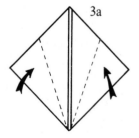

Chapter Thirteen

Food for Thought

Recipes, recipes, and more recipes. I find them everywhere—written on paper napkins and church bulletins, jotted down on backs of supermarket receipts and in phone books, scribbled on bits and pieces of paper. I tuck them in drawers, cupboards, boxes, baskets. And each year I resolve to get them all pulled together and put into some form of book. I do have a proper recipe box—and many cookbooks. Many I've never used, but they're there, just in case I want to use them. I don't know why I collect them with so much gusto, as though the next meal depended on them. It's just something I do.

I have written the preceding chapters with a deep desire that you find practical hints, gentle nudgings, simple suggestions—all to motivate you to get involved in the practice of hospitality. Perhaps you need, along with everything else, the extra impetus of a few more recipes to add to your collection. I could have gone through my pile of recipes and pulled out some special ones for you. But since I am a people person, I instead asked my friends, far and near, to share with us some of their concoctions. The response was overwhelming. The difficulty was in choosing what recipes to include. I had some special criteria. The recipe had to be economical, easy to make, really appealing, and quickly made. I'm not interested in passing on a ho-hum collection.

For those of you who don't know how to cook, I hope you will look at this collection as a way to get started. If you're already a professional, you might find something new that appeals to you. Or maybe you are, like me, in a rut, and just need some fresh recipes.

If you are brand new at this, try putting together a meal based on these recipes. You can change them all you like. Be sure it fits your budget, time frame, home, guests, and most of all, the cook.

BREADS, ROLLS, MUFFINS

Arkansas Monkey Bread

1 can (10) biscuits (the least expensive will be fine)
⅓ c. sugar
½ t. cinnamon
½ c. butter
¾ c. brown sugar
Chopped nuts

Cut each biscuit into fourths, using scissors. Mix the sugar and cinnamon, and roll the cut biscuit pieces in this mixture. Place biscuit squares into a greased bundt pan, sprinkling chopped nuts between layers. Melt the butter and brown sugar together over low heat, then pour this mixture over the biscuit pieces. Top with more chopped nuts. Bake at 400° for 15-20 minutes.

Cousin Juanita Thorne
Rogers, Arkansas

Easy-As-Pie Caramel Rolls

2 pkgs. yeast
1 box yellow cake mix
5 c. flour

In a large bowl dissolve the yeast in 2½ c. warm water. Add the cake mix and flour. Stir well (no kneading necessary). Cover and set in warm place until doubled in size. Cut dough in half, letting one half rest while you work the other. On a floured surface roll dough out into large rectangle; spread with soft butter, brown or white sugar and cinnamon. Then roll up as a jelly roll.

Mix together:

¼ c. butter
½ c. brown sugar
½ c. broken walnut or pecan pieces

Spread this mixture in each of four 9″ round cake pans or two 13″ rectangular pans (a separate mixture is required for each pan). Then cut the dough into 2″ pieces and arrange on top of this mixture. Cover; let rise until double in size (when risen, rolls should touch each other). Bake at 375° until slightly brown (about 20-25 minutes). Turn out onto plate or tray so butter/sugar mixture runs down through the rolls. *These are a delightful combination of cake and bread rolls— and they turn out a lovely yellow color.*

Mabel Danielson, my second mother
Arnold, Maryland

Monterey Bread

1 loaf french bread
1 c. mayonnaise
½ c. chopped onion
½ c. grated Parmesan cheese
½ t. Worcestershire sauce

Split the bread lengthwise. Butter each side. Mix remaining ingredients and spread on both pieces of bread. Sprinkle paprika on top. Toast in oven at 250-300° until hot throughout (5-10 minutes). Use broiler to brown lightly if necessary. Cut into 2-inch pieces to serve.

Betty Thompson
Lompoc, California

Moravian Bread

1 loaf frozen bread dough
2 T. butter
½ c. brown sugar
Dash cinnamon
½ c. chopped walnuts or pecans

Let bread dough rise until double in size. Then cut raised loaf in two. On a floured surface roll each piece into a round, like a pie shell. Place each round in a buttered pie pan, working the dough up along the sides with greased hands. Mix remaining ingredients and sprinkle on each round. Let the rounds rise again until double in bulk. When they have raised, make several indentations in the dough with your thumb to catch the butter as it melts. Bake at 375° until lightly browned (about 10 minutes). Put each round on a plate and cut in wedges with a pizza cutter. Serve immediately. *Best when eaten piping hot.*

Ruth Danielson, my first mother

Bran Muffins

1 c. boiling water
2 c. Kellogg's All-Bran
½ c. shortening
1½ c. sugar
2 beaten eggs
2 c. buttermilk
1 c. Nabisco 100% bran flour
2½ c. flour
2½ t. baking soda
½ t. salt

Mix the All-Bran with boiling water and let stand. Then cream together the shortening and sugar. Add to this mixture the eggs, buttermilk and bran flour. Sift and measure the flour. Then sift again with the baking soda and salt. Fold the soaked All-Bran into the dry ingredients only until moist. Then stir in remaining ingredients. Put in ungreased muffin pans. Bake at 400° for 20-25 minutes. *This dough may be stored for seven weeks in the refrigerator. Take out just what you need for a meal.*

Nancy Huber
Rochester, Minnesota

MAIN DISHES

Savory Rump Roast

One 4-5 lb. beef roast, as lean as you can buy
Chili powder
Carrots
Onions
Potatoes
Celery or cabbage

Brown roast on all sides in oil or Pam. Add small amount of water, cover, and cook slowly for 4 to 4½ hours. (This is best done on top of the stove, but can be done in the oven.) Add a little water as necessary. After about three hours add a dash of chili powder. Then 45 or 50 minutes before serving, add carrot chunks or whole carrots, onions, potatoes (peeled and quartered), and celery or cabbage, whichever you wish. Salt and pepper to taste.

Mary K. O'Daniel
Topeka, Kansas

The Greatest Quick Chicken Casserole Recipe in the World

8 to 10 chicken pieces
1½ c. uncooked rice
2 cans French Onion soup
2 cans cream of mushroom soup
1 small can of mushrooms (optional)

Rinse chicken pieces in cold water. Grease sides and bottom of 9″ × 12″ baking pan or dish. Pour in rice. Add chicken pieces. Salt and pepper to taste. Add mushroom soup and mushrooms. Pour onion soup over all. Bake at 350° for 2 hours. Serves 8 to 10.

Nadal Southern
Commonlife Magazine

Sweet and Sour Chicken Wings

3½ to 4 lbs. chicken wings
Flour seasoned with salt, pepper and ¼ t. curry powder
¾ c. white sugar
½ c. vinegar
¼ c. pineapple juice
¼ c. catsup
1 t. soy sauce
½ t. salt

Separate the chicken wings at the joints; discard the tip section. Roll in the seasoned flour. Brown on both sides in oil, 7 minutes per side. In a medium saucepan, combine remaining ingredients and bring to a boil. Remove from the heat. Arrange browned wings in a 9″ x 13″ pan. Pour mixture over the chicken and bake at 350° for 30 minutes. Turn pieces once to coat with sauce.

Wylma Buckles
Roseville, Minnesota

Mexican Style Steamed Fish

2 T. vegetable oil
½ of 6-oz. can frozen orange juice concentrate
¼ c. lemon juice
1 small onion, grated
Salt and pepper, to taste
Cayenne powder
2 lbs. frozen fish fillets

Arrange fish fillets in a 12″ x 8″ glass dish. Combine remaining ingredients and pour over fish. Add 6 sprigs of cilantro (Mexican coriander) leaves. (Adds a truly delightful flavor.) Cover, but vent at the corners. Cook in oven or microwave on high for 8-10 minutes. *A quick meal served with rice.*

Jean Buker
Wheaton, Illinois

Left-Over Mashed Potatoes

4 c. mashed potatoes
2 egg yolks
Salt and pepper to taste
Dash of flour
2 stiffly beaten egg whites

Mix the mashed potatoes, egg yolks, salt, pepper, and flour by hand. Then fold in the stiffly beaten egg whites. Fluff it into a casserole and if desired, top with grated cheese. Bake at 350° for 15-20 minutes. *Believe it or not, this is good enough for company and easy to serve.*

Connie Johnson
Shikarpur, Pakistan

Salisbury Steaks

1 lb. hamburger
⅓ c. catsup
½ t. dry mustard
1 to 2 t. Worcestershire sauce
1 c. bread crumbs
¼ c. evaporated milk
Salt and pepper, to taste
1 large onion

Slice onion into 5 or 6 thick slices. Brown in a little grease and remove from pan. Combine remaining ingredients and shape into 5 or 6 large patties. Brown on each side in a little grease over high heat. Arrange patties in a baking dish, placing one onion slice on each patty. Finish cooking in a 350° oven for 30 minutes. *For a main meal, serve with baked potatoes, or can be used with big buns.*

Polly Brown
Shikarpur, Pakistan

Egg and Cheese Strata

12 slices white bread
Butter or margarine
Mustard
12 oz. grated sharp cheddar cheese
6 eggs
4½ c. milk

Trim off the bread crusts. Butter each slice of bread on one side; spread mustard on the other. Stack and cut into cubes. Place cubes in a 9″ x 13″ pan. Sprinkle the grated cheese over the bread cubes. Separate the eggs. Beat the yolks, adding the milk and beating until frothy. Beat the whites until stiff. Fold into the egg yolk mixture. Pour over cheese and bread cubes and bake at 350° for 1 hour. *I have no idea where this came from. If it's yours, you can have the glory.*

Zucchini Casserole

5 medium zucchini
¾ c. onion, chopped
1 c. croutons
1 can cream of chicken soup
½ c. milk
½ c. sour cream

Cut zucchini in thick slices and boil until just tender. Drain and combine with remaining ingredients in a baking pan. Bake at 350° for 30 minutes. Serves 10 or more.

Jo Davis
Monett, Missouri

Easy-Serve Spaghetti

1 or 2 lbs. spaghetti
2 pkgs. Mozzarella cheese, shredded or sliced
Your favorite spaghetti and meatball sauce (any kind will do)

Cook spaghetti according to package directions. Drain and rinse. Place in a slightly greased 9″ × 13″ pan. Cover with cheese. Place in a moderate oven just until the cheese is melted and spaghetti is warmed. To serve, cut into squares while in the pan and add sauce at the table. Or, you can spread the sauce on top, and cut the whole business into squares. *Great for a large crowd; much easier to serve than regular spaghetti. Can be made ahead of time and refrigerated, even frozen.*

Barbara Yearick
Monterrey, Mexico

Calico Beans

1 lg. can baked beans
1 can butter beans, drained
1 can red kidney beans, not drained
1 medium onion, chopped
¾ c. brown sugar
¼ c. vinegar
1 T. dry mustard
½ t. ginger
4 slices crisply fried bacon

Mix all together and bake at 350° for 1½ hours.

Faith Finley
Cambridge, Minnesota

SALADS

Creative Fresh Vegetable Salad

4 c. raw cauliflower, cubed or flowerlets
4 c. raw broccoli, cubed or flowerlets

Mix together, then add bacon bits, nuts, small cubes of cheese, or anything you think you want.

Dressing

¾ c. mayonnaise
¼ c. yogurt
Salt and pepper to taste

I also add onion powder, garlic salt, Season-All, parsley flakes; almost anything I find in my cupboard. Pour over salad just before serving. Sprinkle with sunflower seeds, paprika, or Parmesan cheese. *This is my own recipe, but I'm sure I got it from someone else originally. Its best advertisement is that when I take it to any kind of potluck, which I always do, there is never any left.*

Calico Cabbage Slaw

4 c. shredded cabbage
1 c. cubed Colby cheese
1 12-oz. can whole kernel corn with red and green sweet peppers, drained
2 T. sliced black olives

Dressing

1 c. salad dressing or mayonnaise
2 T. sugar
2 T. vinegar
1 T. prepared mustard
½ t. dill weed

Combine dressing ingredients and pour over combined salad ingredients. Chill. Can be made the day before. Makes 5 cups.

Jan Long
New Brighton, Minnesota

Macie Salad

1 lg. pkg. of lime Jell-O

Dissolve with 2 c. of hot water and 1 c. of cold water. Let set until slightly thickened.

Add:

1 can crushed pineapple, with juice
1 c. chopped nuts
1 c. cottage cheese

Mix ingredients well into the Jell-O. Then add 1 c. soft Dream Whip or whipped cream.

Macie Mansfield
A childhood babysitter

Hot Chicken Salad

2 c. chicken, cooked and cubed
1 c. celery, finely cut
½ c. slivered almonds
½ c. mayonnaise
1 c. cream of chicken soup
1 t. chopped onion
1 T. lemon juice
2 hardboiled eggs, chopped

Combine all ingredients in a casserole dish. Top with ½ c. crushed potato chips. Bake at 375° for 20-25 minutes. (One large chicken makes four cups of cooked meat.)

Wylma Buckles
Roseville, Minnesota

Vegetable Salad

1 can very young petite peas
1 can Green Giant shoe peg white corn
1 can french-cut green beans
1 small jar pimiento, chopped
1 green pepper, finely diced
1 c. green onions, chopped with the greens

Dressing

½ c. oil
¾ c. sugar
1 t. salt
½ t. pepper
1 T. water
¾ c. vinegar

Bring dressing ingredients to a boil and boil until sugar is dissolved. Cool. Pour dressing over the vegetables and let stand 2 hours or longer. Drain. Reserve juice for leftovers.

DRINKS AND SNACKS

Double Berry Punch

8 c. cranberry juice cocktail, chilled
3 c. raspberry-flavored carbonated beverage, chilled
1 10-oz. pkg. frozen raspberries, thawed
1 qt. raspberry sherbet

Pour all except the carbonated beverage over sherbet. Add raspberries. Add carbonated beverage just before serving.

Cindy's Punch

3 c. sugar
6 c. water

Boil for 3 minutes and cool.

Add:

1 12-oz. frozen orange juice
2 bananas, mashed
¼ c. Real Lemon Juice
1 c. unsweetened pineapple juice

Mix these ingredients and then freeze in large plastic container. When ready to serve, add five 1-qt. bottles of ginger ale to frozen mixture. Makes 48 5-oz. servings.

Cindy Trulson
Storm Lake, Iowa

Northwestern College Punch

1 qt. vanilla ice cream
3 qts. lemon sherbet
1 42-oz. can apricot nectar
1 lg. bottle 7-Up

Mix ice cream and sherbet in large punch bowl. Add nectar until slushy. Then add 7-Up just before serving. This recipe can be varied, using almost any kind of ice cream, sherbet, and juice. Mint and lime sherbets make a real treat. Serves 25 or 30.

Grace's Favorite

Put 3 or 4 ice cubes in each of your best goblets

Then add:

⅓ glass of sugarless pink lemonade
⅓ glass cranberry juice cocktail
⅓ glass ginger ale

It is tangy, delicious, cooling, and beautiful to look at. Have plenty on hand. They will come back for more.

Cocktail Meatballs

1 lb. ground beef
½ c. dry bread crumbs
⅓ c. minced onion
¼ c. milk
1 egg
1 T. snipped parsley
1 t. salt
⅛ t. pepper
½ t. Worcestershire sauce
¼ c. shortening
1 12-oz. bottle chili sauce
1 10-oz. jar grape jelly

Mix ground beef, bread crumbs, onion, milk, egg and next four ingredients. Gently shape into 1″ balls. Melt shortening in large skillet; brown meatballs. Remove; pour off fat. Heat chili sauce and jelly in skillet, stirring constantly until jelly is melted. Add meatballs and stir until thoroughly coated. Simmer uncovered for 30 minutes. Makes 5 dozen. For variety, substitute 4 jars (½ oz. each) cocktail sausages for meatballs. This works great in a chafing dish or slow cooker. Be sure to supply sturdy sticks for easy eating.

Betty Crocker Cookbook

Oyster Cracker Munchies

2 pkgs. Keebler Oyster Crackers
2 pkgs. Ranch House dressing mix (dry)
1 bottle Orville Redenbacher oil

Mix all together (yes, you should use the full bottle of oil). Stir often until oil is absorbed. *This will NOT be greasy, believe it or not.*

Barbara Yearick
Monterrey, Mexico

Chinese Glazed Triscuits (low sodium)

¼ c. brown sugar, firmly packed
2 T. unsalted margarine, softened
¼ t. dried orange peel
¼ t. 5-spice powder (see recipe below)
¼ t. low-sodium soy sauce (Kikoman Lite)
⅛ t. onion powder
24 low-salt Triscuits
24 whole, unsalted walnut halves

In a small bowl, thoroughly blend brown sugar, margarine, dried orange peel, 5-spice powder, lite soy sauce and onion powder. Spread ¼ t. of mixture on each cracker. Place one walnut half on each glazed Triscuit. Arrange appetizers in single layer, walnut side up on microwave plate. Microwave 2 minutes on medium power, rotating after 1 minute. Or bake at 350° for 5 minutes. Cool before serving. Makes 24 appetizers. (Items 4, 5, and 7 can be found in the Low Sodium section of supermarket. Made to order for those on low sodium diets, and those not on low sodium diets will love them, too.)

5-Spice Powder

1 t. ground cinnamon
1 t. crushed aniseed
¼ t. crushed fennel seed
¼ t. freshly ground pepper or Szechwan pepper
⅛ t. ground cloves

Combine and store in covered container. Can be used for other dishes as well.

Mt. Sinai Hospital Hypertension Program
Minneapolis, Minnesota

Tangy Cheese Ball

1 2-lb. brick Velveeta cheese
2 lbs. sharp cheddar cheese
1 8-oz. pkg. cream cheese (for softer ball, add 1 more 4-oz. pkg.)

Shred cheeses together and mix thoroughly with wooden spoon or hands.

Then add:

1 jar pimientos, ground up with one large onion. (I use my food processor.) Or, put pimientos and onion pieces in blender, cover with cold water, then run on *grind* for several seconds. Drain liquid, then add to cheese mixture. Can also add to taste: pinch of garlic salt or garlic juice; shot of Tabasco sauce; shot of Worcestershire sauce; ground nuts; bacon bits; parsley flakes—whatever you like. Be creative. Mix thoroughly with cheeses, then press into 4 large balls. Roll each ball in crushed pecans or walnuts. Wrap each ball in plastic wrap and refrigerate. For a harder, more crumbly ball, use more hard cheese, or cut down on soft cheese. *This is my own recipe. I made enough one year to sell at a craft fair.*

SPECIAL SOUPS

Hearty Vegetable Soup

1 lb. ground beef
1 clove garlic
1 medium onion, sliced.

Brown together and drain.

Add:

1 c. shredded cabbage
4 c. fresh or canned tomatoes
1 c. sliced celery
1 c. sliced carrots
1 can whole kernel corn w/liquid
1 can kidney beans w/liquid
4 c. water
½ c. red cooking wine
1 t. seasoned salt
1 t. Italian seasoning
1 t. salt

Simmer for at least one hour. Flavors blend better if made ahead of time. Serves 6 to 8.

Helen Lewis
Arden Hills, Minnesota

Salmon Chowder

½ c. chopped onion
½ c. chopped green pepper

Sauté, then add:

2 c. diced potatoes
10 oz. frozen mixed vegetables
2½ c. chicken broth

Simmer 12 minutes or until vegetables are tender, then add:

1 can red salmon (15½ oz.)
1 can cream-style corn (8½ oz.)
3 c. whole milk
½ c. Half and Half
½ t. salt
⅛ t. pepper
½ t. celery seed
½ t. dill weed

Bring to a simmer but do not boil. When serving, add fresh chopped parsley.

Esther Edwards
known as the "Soup Queen" of Wheaton
Wheaton, Illinois

Chunky Lentil Soup

1 lb. lean ground chuck
1 c. dried lentils, well rinsed and sorted
1 c. diced, pared carrots
1 c. chopped onion
1 c. chopped cabbage
1 t. finely chopped green pepper
1 t. salt
½ t. pepper
1 bay leaf
2 beef boullion cubes
1 46-oz. can tomato sauce (5½ cups)
4 c. water

Cook ground chuck in 6-qt. Dutch oven over medium heat until well browned. Drain off all fat. Stir in remaining ingredients. Cook over high heat until mixture comes to boil. Reduce heat to low and simmer for 1½ hours, or until lentils are tender. Best to cover it. This is great frozen, great to take to sick people. Add salad and dessert and it makes a whole meal. *Scrumptious!*

Farm Journal

Hardy Cheddar Chowder

3 c. chicken broth
4 medium potatoes, diced
1 medium onion, diced
1 c. sliced carrots
½ c. diced green pepper
⅓ c. oleo or butter
⅓ c. flour
4 c. milk
3 c. grated sharp cheddar cheese
¼ t. hot pepper sauce

Combine chicken broth and vegetables; simmer 12 minutes. Melt oleo or butter. Blend in flour. Gradually add milk. Cook, stirring constantly until thickened slightly. Combine with broth and vegetables. Add grated sharp cheddar cheese and hot pepper sauce. Stir over medium heat until cheese melts. Do not boil.

Esther Edwards
Wheaton, Illinois

FOREIGN DISHES

Chicken Curry (for the "uninitiated")

1 or 2 lb. chicken, cut into pieces (best when skinned)
2 lg. onions, sliced
2 t. ground coriander
¼ t. garlic salt
¼ t. ground ginger
⅛ t. ground red pepper
½ t. ground tumeric
½ c. yogurt
4 oz. butter
1 bay leaf
Salt to taste

Sauté onions in butter until golden brown. Add ½ c. water and all the spices. Stir mixture until water evaporates. Add chicken and brown. Then add yogurt and ½ c. water. Simmer in covered pan until sauce thickens and chicken is tender. More water may be added if necessary. Serve over rice.

Topping:

Sauté 1 c. raisins, and/or 1 finely chopped onion (sauté until onions are crispy), and/or chopped green pepper, and/or 1 c. peanuts. Put toppings in separate bowls.

Pakistan Embassy
Washington, D.C.

Arabic Salad

1 lg. onion
2 lg. cucumbers
3 tomatoes
15 fresh mint leaves
2 fresh limes
2 T. salad oil
Salt and pepper

Chop onions, cucumbers, and tomatoes. Add the mint leaves whole. Mix, cover, and refrigerate an hour, or overnight. In a cup, mix the juice of limes and the oil, salt and pepper. Have ready to serve with salad just before bringing to the table.

Ruth Montgomery
Karachi, Pakistan
Formerly of Ramalah, Jordan

Chili Con Queso (Hot Cheese Dip)

2 lb. Kraft American cheese
1 can whole tomatoes (28 oz.)
1 can Ortega diced green chilis (4 oz.)
1 T. instant minced onion flakes
1 t. LaVictoria Salsa Jalapena

After draining whole tomatoes, place in double boiler, fondue dish or electric saucepan and chop finely with inverted tomato can. Slice the cheese into ½" cubes and combine with tomatoes, diced green chilis, minced onion flakes and Salsa Jalapena. Stir frequently while heating to a simmer. Serve hot after the cheese cubes have melted. *Great for dipping raw vegetables, chips, tortillas, etc.*

Mabel Wilkins
Sepulveda, California

Java Chicken and Rice

Chicken breasts boiled, boned, and cubed (2 breasts serves 3)
Chicken broth
Sliced green onions
Crushed pineapple
Cheddar cheese (grated)
Raisins
Shredded Coconut
Sliced almonds (or walnuts or peanuts)

Arrange all ingredients in separate bowls. Can be set out buffet style so each can make his own combination. Can all be used as a topping for fluffy white rice. Put hot chicken broth in pitcher to be poured over top. This melts the cheese. With a roll and salad, it makes a meal. This basic recipe can also be used with ground beef or beef cubes. *It is a favorite meal at Ivory Coast Academy in Bouake, Ivory Coast.*

Grace Elkins
St. Helens, Oregon

Speeha (An Arabic baked sandwich)

2 loaves frozen bread dough
1 c. finely chopped onion
1 lb. ground beef
⅔ c. yogurt or vinegar
Salt and pepper

Combine ground beef and yogurt with the finely chopped onion. Salt and pepper generously and knead with the hands for 2 minutes. Cover and set aside in refrigerator for at least an hour. Let 2 loaves of frozen bread dough rise until double. Melt shortening in two 9" x 12" cake pans. Pinch off 2"-balls of dough, shape as for hamburger rolls, and turn in the melted shortening. (12 in a pan leaves space between.) When all are shaped in pans, flatten each with the hand until they touch. Put a generously heaped T. of the cold mixture on top of each bun. If pine nuts are available, put 5 on each meat patty. Bake for an hour in preheated oven at 400°. *Best served warm.*

Ruth Montgomery
Karachi, Pakistan

Persian Chicken

4 boned chicken breasts
¼ c. flour
1 t. seasoned salt
¼ t. chili powder
⅛ t. pepper
⅛ t. ground cumin
3 T. oil
¾ c. dry white wine
1 c. bulgar wheat
2 T. sliced green onions
2 T. butter or margarine
2 c. chicken broth
½ t. salt
¼ t. thyme
1 green pepper, seeded and chunked
2 large bananas, peeled and chunked
¼ c. dairy sour cream

Wipe breasts and pat dry. Combine flour, seasoned salt, chili powder, pepper and cumin. Coat chicken breasts with this mixture and brown well in oil in large skillet. Add wine, cover and simmer until tender, about 20 minutes. Meanwhile, sauté wheat and green onions in butter until golden. Add chicken broth, salt and thyme. Cover and bring to boil. Reduce heat; simmer 15 minutes. Spoon wheat onto serving platter. Arrange chicken on wheat; keep warm in oven. Add green pepper chunks to drippings in chicken pan. Cover and simmer about 8 minutes until tender. Sprinkle green pepper over chicken. Add banana chunks to skillet. Cook until heated through. Arrange banana chunks around chicken. Stir sour cream into skillet. Heat but do not boil. Pour over chicken platter and serve. *I found this recipe in our own suburban newspaper.*

INDIAN AND PAKISTANI BREAD VARIATIONS

Chapatis

1 c. unsifted unbleached white flour
1 c. whole wheat flour
½ t. salt
2 T. peanut oil
½ to ¾ c. water

Combine flours, salt, oil and ½ c. water (add more water, a teaspoon at a time, if dough is still crumbly). Knead dough, then let rest 30 minutes. Break into 12 parts; keep unused dough balls under plastic wrap. Work with one ball at a time, pressing the ball flat between hands. Sprinkle a little flour on board then use rolling pin to roll flattened ball into a 6" circle about ⅛" thick. Use as little flour as possible when rolling. Heat griddle until drop of water dances on surface. Place dough on griddle for about 30 seconds. Turn over with tongs and leave for 30 or more seconds, moving constantly with fingers or shaking pan back and forth. Notice that this is all done on a dry griddle. Dough will puff up as it cooks. Use a clean cloth to push down bubbles.

Puris

Use same dough as above, same process. Fry each round in about 1-½" hot peanut oil. When bubbly on one side, turn carefully with large spatula to other side. They become crispy and puffed up like pillows. Drain on paper towel, then serve.

DESSERTS

Arkansas Poor Boy Cobbler

1 c. all purpose flour
1 c. white sugar
⅔ t. baking powder
¼ t. salt
1 stick margarine
1 egg
Fruit
Spices

In a square pan, mix together the flour, sugar, baking powder, and salt. Add one stick melted margarine and one well-beaten egg. Mix together thoroughly. Pour over this any kind of juicy fruit such as peaches, sweetened to taste. Add any spices fruit may need. Bake at 350° for 45 minutes or until dough is done in the middle. The dough surfaces as the cobbler cooks. For peaches, nutmeg and almond flavoring really enhance the flavor.

Juanita Thorne
Rogers, Arkansas

Praline Pear Gingerbread

1 can (16 oz.) Bartlett pear halves
1 pkg. gingerbread mix
3 T. melted butter or margarine
½ c. chopped nuts
1 T. heavy cream

Drain pears, reserve syrup. Bake gingerbread using pear syrup in place of water. Place pear halves on top of baked gingerbread. Combine remaining ingredients; spoon over pear halves and gingerbread. Broil 4″ from heat, 3 minutes or until bubbly.

Helen Lewis
Arden Hills, Minnesota

Pineapple Dessert

1 20-oz. can crushed pineapple
1½ c. coconut
1 box yellow cake mix
1 c. margarine or butter
1 c. chopped pecans
Whipped cream or Cool Whip

Lightly butter 9″ x 13″ pan. Spread in pan crushed pineapple and juice. Spread coconut on pineapple; sprinkle cake mix on top of coconut and dot with margarine. Sprinkle with chopped pecans. Bake at 350° for 30-50 minutes. Serve with a dollop of whipped cream.

Bea Kenter

Lemon Freeze

2 eggs, separated
1 can condensed milk
⅓ c. lemon juice
½ t. lemon rind
2 T. sugar
¾ c. crushed cookies or corn flakes
¼ c. margarine

Beat egg yolks until thick. Add milk, lemon juice and rind. Beat egg whites. Add 2 T. sugar. Fold into first mixture. Pour into crumb crust made from the crushed cookies or cornflakes (mix with ¼ c. melted margarine). Freeze; cut into squares. Garnish each with dollop of Dream Whip and a cherry, or crushed nuts.

Chocolate Topped Date Cake

1 c. chopped dates
1¼ c. boiling water
1 t. baking soda
¾ c. shortening
1 c. sugar
2 eggs
1½ c. flour
¼ t. salt
1 6-oz. pkg. chocolate chips
1 T. sugar
½ c. chopped nuts

Put dates in bowl and cover with boiling water to which you have added the soda. Let stand to cool. Cream shortening and sugar together until fluffy, beat in eggs. Sift flour and salt into creamed mixture; mix well. Stir in cooled date mixture. Spread in a greased 9″ x 13″ baking pan. Sprinkle the chocolate chips, sugar and nut meats over the batter. Bake at 350° for about 30 minutes, or until cake springs back when touched lightly. Serve warm with ice cream or whipped cream, or cool and cut into small squares.

Betty Thompson
Lompoc, California

Verna's Kringle Recipe

1 c. flour
½ c. butter
1½ T. water

Cut together like pie crust dough and pat into round pan (pizza pan is fine). This is sticky dough, so putting plastic wrap over it before patting makes it easier.

Topping:

1 c. water
½ c. butter
1 c. flour
3 eggs
Pinch of salt
1 t. almond extract

Boil together water and butter. Then add flour, stirring immediately until blended. Add eggs, one at a time, salt, and almond extract. Bake at 350° for one hour. Frost with powdered sugar icing with almond extract. Add nuts and maraschino cherries or whatever for decoration. *Don't forget the almond extract—it is the crowning touch and taste. Perfect for morning coffee or afternoon tea.*

Verna Halvorson
Shoreview, Minnesota

Sanford Hospital Sugar Cookies

1 cup each:
Powdered sugar
Granulated sugar
Margarine
Vegetable oil

Mix together and add:

2 eggs
1 t. vanilla
4½ c. flour (no more)
½ t. each: salt, soda, cream of tartar

Blend well; make into 1″ balls. Flatten with bottom of glass dipped in sugar. Bake on ungreased cookie sheet for 15 minutes in 350° oven. Make as big or as small as you like—the bigger the better. *They melt in your mouth!*

Sanford Hospital
Farmington, Minnesota

World's Greatest Apple Dumplings

2 c. sugar
2 c. water
1 t. cinnamon
¼ t. nutmeg
¼ c. butter

Make into a syrup, boil about 3 minutes. Using 6 apples, peel, core, and cut into quarters.

2 c. flour
1 t. salt
2 t. baking powder
¾ c. shortening
½ c. milk

Cut together to make dough. Roll out dough to ¼″ thickness. Cut into 5″ squares. Place 4 apple pieces into each square of dough. Bring corners of dough piece to center, making a secure ball. Place dumplings in baking dish. Pour syrup over the top and bake at 375° for 35-40 minutes. Top with whipped cream or ice cream. *Don't expect to have any left—these melt in your mouth! My husband's mother was famous in her part of the country for these scrumptious dumplings.*

Kate Pittman
Monett, Missouri

When I worked through these recipes from friends all over the world, I was impressed by our conveniences. It's simple to go to the store at any moment and buy the things we need—and recipes have been made unbelievably easy for us. To be able to start with frozen bread dough, a cake mix, or a spaghetti mix greatly simplifies cooking. I can't imagine how anyone could ever use the excuse, "I just don't know how to cook."

As I've written, I have remembered what it was like when we first arrived as missionaries in Pakistan. All over the world, missionary mothers cook the same way our ancestors did in this country. If you think it's hard to muster up the energy in this country to bake cookies, cakes, or prepare a meal, try this one:

Missionary Mother's Cake

Prepare fire in mud stove. Pull utensils out of storage box and rinse with boiled water. Check flour for bugs. Measure and sift 2 c. flour, ¼ t. salt and ½ t. baking powder into bowl. Stop to kill cockroach crawling across the table. Prepare powdered milk and add 1 c. to mixture. Add 2 eggs. (Oops, no eggs left.) Call Johnny and have him fetch 2 eggs from tribal neighbors. Stir milk and dry ingredients until batter is smooth. Johnny returns with eggs. Oh, no. They're duck eggs. Add eggs anyhow—after all, who's going to know? Add 2 t. lemon juice for flavoring. Oh, no. All lemons have been picked by villagers. Substitute papaya juice. Put in greased pan and sprinkle with palm nuts. Bake on mud stove until cake rises and when pricked, knife comes out clean. Serves a family of 6, provided supper is not shared with the rest of the village.

Mrs. Joy Benzio, Trans-World Radio Headquarters

Bibliography

Aldrich, Joseph. *Lifestyle Evangelism*. Portland, Oreg.: Multnomah Press, 1981.

Better Homes and Gardens editors. *Better Homes and Gardens Cooking for Two*. Des Moines, Iowa: Better Homes and Gardens Books.

Better Homes and Gardens editors. *Better Homes and Gardens Meals for One or Two*. Des Moines, Iowa: Better Homes and Gardens Books.

Bornstedt, Marianne Von & Ulla Prytz. *Folding Table Napkins*. New York: Sterling Publishing Co., 1968.

Collins, Marjorie A. *Who Cares About the Missionary?* Winona Lake, Ind.: Don Wardell, 1982.

Cornell, Jane. *The Art of Table Decoration*. New York: The Warner Lifestyle Library, 1980.

Dlugosch, Sharon. *Folding Table Napkins: A New Look at a Traditional Craft*. New Brighton, Minn.: Brighton Publications, 1980.

Dlugosch, Sharon. *Table Setting Guide*. New Brighton, Minn.: Brighton Publications, 1982.

Doering, Jeanne. *The Power of Encouragement*. Chicago: Moody Press, 1983.

Eaves, John. *Commonlife*, Vol. 4, #1, p. 14. Grace Haven Ministry Center, Rt. 10, Woodville Rd., Mansfield, Ohio 44903.

Felton, Sandra. *The Messie's Manual*. Miami Springs, Fla.: Writer's Service, 1981.

Hoke, Stephen. "Culture Shock." Pasadena, Calif.: *World Christian* magazine, November/December, 1984, pp. 26-28.

LeFever, Marlene D. *Creative Hospitality*. Wheaton, Ill.: Tyndale House Publishers, 1980.

Little, Paul. *A Guide to International Friendship*. Downers Grove, Ill.: Inter-Varsity Press, 1959.

Mains, Karen Burton. *Open Heart, Open Home*. Elgin, Ill.: David C. Cook Publishing, 1980.

Neff, David. "Bad Thoughts." *HIS* magazine, April 1985, p. 32.

Palfenier, Jerry. *An MK's Handbook*. Judson Baptist College.

Pillsbury editors. *Pillsbury Kitchens' Family Cookbook*. New York: Doubleday.

Pippert, Rebecca Manley. *Out of the Salt Shaker & Into the World*. Downers Grove, Ill.: InterVarsity Press, 1979.

Rombauer, Irma S. and Marion R. Becker. *The Joy of Cooking*. New York: Bobbs-Merrill, 1975.

Sunset Casserole Cookbook. *Sunset* magazine.

Steps to Salvation

1. God is all wise and the only one who can show you the purpose and meaning of life.

2. God is holy and cannot approve of sin. He will judge and condemn all wrongdoing.

3. God is also merciful. He offers forgiveness to all who will turn from running their own lives and receive His Son, Jesus Christ, as their Lord and Savior (1 John 1:9). Jesus is the only way to God for He said, "I am the way, the truth, and the life; no man cometh unto the Father, but by me" (John 14:6).

4. Those who put their trust in Jesus Christ will have forgiveness of sins, fulfillment of life here and heaven in the world to come. Those who do not receive God's mercy and love remain under His judgment. "He that believeth on the Son hath everlasting life: and he that believeth not the Son shall not see life; but the wrath of God abideth on him" (John 3:36).

5. God proved His love by giving His Son to die for your sins. How are *you* responding to God's love for you as expressed in Jesus Christ's death and resurrection?

6. Are you *unconcerned*? Even if you do not care at all about God, He still loves you and Jesus Christ still died for your sins (Romans 5:8).

7. Are you *concerned* about your sins and anxious to do something about them?

8. True concern will lead you to *conviction*—knowing that you are a sinner and separated from God by your sins. "For all have sinned and come short of the glory of God" (Romans 3:23).

9. When your sins bother you remember that God the Holy Spirit is trying to persuade you to *repent* and turn your life over to Him.

10. Repentance is a deep change of heart and mind which leads you to forsake all known sin and the right to run your life independently of God. It is a spiritual U-turn necessary before you believe. Jesus said, "Except ye repent, ye shall all likewise perish" (Luke 13:3).

11. When you make a commitment of all that you are and have to the total rule of the Lord Jesus Christ, He will save you from eternal separation from God. "If thou shalt confess with thy mouth the LORD Jesus, and shalt believe in thine heart that God hath raised him from the dead, thou shalt be saved" (Romans 10:9).

12. When you completely surrender to the Lordship of Christ, you will become a member of God's family, and be spiritually reborn. "Except a man be born again, he cannot see the kingdom of God" (John 3:3).

13. Are you willing to ask Jesus Christ to come into your life as Lord and Savior? If so, then in your own words talk to God and . . .

    _____Confess your sins—call them by name.

    _____Tell God you are repenting, willing to forsake all known sin and the right to run your life independently of Him.

    _____Tell God you are believing in Him, giving yourself entirely to Him, and receiving Jesus Christ as Lord into your life.

14. God will keep His Word, give the forgiveness you ask, and receive you. "These things have I written unto you that believe on the name of the Son of God; that ye may know that ye have eternal life" (1 John 5:13).

Adapted from *Step Up to Life* by Elmer H. Murdoch (Bethany House Publishers, 1971).